Debor…

THE EXTRAORDINARY LIFE OF AN ORDINARY MAN

Surviving When Life Sucks

Wishing you the Best of Health!

A Memoir

Dr. Tom Schneider, M.D.

Tom S. MD

Ballast Books

Ballast Books, LLC
Washington, DC
www.ballastbooks.com

ISBN 978-1-7334280-8-8

Library of Congress Control Number has been applied for

Published by Ballast Books
www.ballastbooks.com

For more information, bulk orders, appearances or speaking requests, please email info@ballastbooks.com

Thanks, Umpy

Table of Contents

This story is true. Not "based on a true story." It's my entirely true story, without exaggerations or deceit. In that regard, it's a rare memoir because everything spoken or written today seems to be filled with spin, better known as "bull."

But from a broader perspective, this history is about all of us. My disasters and tribulations are yours as well. You have had to survive, or might still be surviving, turmoil galore. And whether you're battling illness, divorce, or business failure, they all take their toll. So the "why" of this book is simply to show how we are all in this thing called life, together. I am hoping my emotions will be yours. My failures, yours. Your challenges will, of course, be far different from mine, but the gut-wrenching feeling of despair is identical for us. I hope that relating to these potholes of mine will be like vicarious teaching for you. Why?

Because we're all in this together. May you learn with little pain.

Introduction

"The ultimate measure of a man is not where he stands in moments of comfort and convenience, but where he stands at times of challenge and controversy."

-M.L. King, Jr.

The shaking was becoming uncontrollable. Around me in the pitch blackness, I could make out the chin-high water rippling through the rice paddies. It was tar-dark wherever I scanned. And yet the moonless evening sky was crowded with stars, like a stuffed cherry pie. Food was creeping into my mind. The tremors I was noticing were the visible evidence of the physical shock coursing through my battered body. I looked up to the heavens and grabbed a moment of calm watching those endless stars over Vietnam. They pulsed and glowed through my tears. I was losing it.

It had been about eight hours since I had been shot down in Huê, along the North-South Vietnam border, with no sign of rescue yet in sight. As I shook with injury and sickness, I wondered if I would ever get out of there. Or was I destined to die in the flooded farmlands of Vietnam like so many of my fellow pilots and countrymen? Then, as my thoughts were near their bleakest, I thought of words my grandmother had spoken to me some 15 years earlier.

"Tommy," she had told me on that cold winter morning from her house in Vermont, "You need to take care of yourself. Don't count on others, ever. Be strong. You can do it all, my grandson." She wiped away my tears. I had felt ten feet tall.

The memory strengthened me. I got pissed. I decided, then and there, I was going to get through this. Whatever it took, I would make it out of Vietnam, alive.

And I did. Thanks, Grandma. I'll never forget you or your words.

Chapter One

The Agent Orange Country Club

"Some things never leave you no matter how hard you cry."

\- Me

I should have known back on May 23, 1945, that the first slap on my bottom by the delivering doctor would be only the first of many to come. The day I got shot down wasn't the first time—and wouldn't be the last—that I would have to rely on my grandmother's prophetic words. But it was one of the most memorable moments. Like your first kiss.

It started out as a regular sweltering day during the height of the Vietnam War in 1969. The day sucked, from the moment I tried to scarf down some dry scrambled eggs and sausage from the mess hall. A far cry from my grandma's favorite bacon and biscuits that I remembered from boyhood back in Rutland, Vermont. But the dehydrated eggs were at least filling for a quivering stomach. I'm not sure how Clint Eastwood can look so cool in his tough-guy scenes, because I sure as hell never could.

The war in Vietnam was an everyday nightmare. I was a Navy pilot flying combat missions over South Vietnam in an F-4 Phantom. Frightened and scared weren't sudden emotions that crept momentarily into each and every day. They were the status quo, but of course no one could admit that, not even to themselves. Ever been so cold and wet you felt the weather in your bones? That's how deep the terror went. But you learned to swagger and hang a Marlboro cigarette off your lower lip. Your face and swaggering walk said to all of your crew and fellow pilots, "Yes, I am a true badass!" The only one who knew it was all crap was you.

Thunderous noise, bells, whistles, and loudspeakers blaring were the cacophony of aircraft launches from a carrier. No way to hear your stomach's gurgle from the dry eggs and sausage. But the smell! No one who has lived an aircraft carrier life ever forgets the smell of JP-4 jet-engine fuel wafting through the air. It was a narcotic. It enhanced your fear but kept bringing you back, like a wicked lover.

As for me, once I was airborne and had glanced down at the aircraft carrier falling behind me, I was always taken by how small it was and getting smaller as I climbed to altitude. Did I actually have to land back on that little postage stamp? It reminded me of the Revell plastic models I had built as a young boy. But it wasn't plastic and it wasn't a model. It was home. It was another gut-wrenching gauntlet to deal with after the mission.

When we returned from a mission, all of us had learned to walk and look like members of the aforementioned badass club. I don't know what my comrades did when on board and back in their cramped, smelly cabins, but as for me, I hit the head for a mandatory and uncontrollable bowel movement. I'm not sure even the real Clint could fake it. Then, time to hit the rack after a dinner of mystery meat and mashed potatoes from an ersatz gourmet buffet.

The glamour of a Navy pilot in war was a crock of crap. And what a mind game. We were playing a political game for men who were cutting into a filet mignon at the 1789 Restaurant in Georgetown, D.C. All of us knew of hostile hit sites to attack in Vietnam, but we were ordered to stand down. Politics, corruption, and money all ruled the war, and then there was my favorite aspect. This morass, with a pulse of Agent Orange. This delightful toxin was used as a defoliant. The bad news is that it never leaves the universe; it's still in Vietnam. Over time, it is responsible for diabetes, cancer, heart disease, kidney failure, and a host of other lovelies. Why was it my favorite disaster of the war? Because later that day I would have the joy of taking an unscheduled swim in a rice paddy laced with Agent Orange. The real karma of that? I had probably dropped that toxic poison. And it would come back to haunt and scourge me for the rest of my life.

My flight that day was routine. Not! No such thing. My RIO "backseat" navigator or, kiddingly, GIB (guy in back) was Ben Baron. A good-looking guy from Sacramento, he was actually the brains for our flights. I just pulled the stick forward and houses would get big. Stick back, and houses got small. Ben scanned the sky and radar for bogeys (enemy planes and hot sticks or missiles). Great guy, and I more than miss him today. Smooth air and CAVU (Ceiling and Visibility Unlimited). Quiet day. Ben could snooze. He didn't.

BOOM! My starboard wing was gone. A nicely placed ground-to-air missile had found its mark. Me. Whoever said that "Charlie" (North Vietnamese soldiers) needed glasses? Damn, they were good and so committed. And we were going down. "Eject, eject, eject!" I shouted into the mic. All I recall after that was floating down into a rice paddy. Actually, we called the parachute ejection "hitting the silk elevator," and I don't remember any of it. Landing waist-deep in rice muck woke me from my stupor. Years later, I would learn that my stupor had been shock. We had been electronically warned of hot sticks launched in the zone, but we had been here before, so merely took another chance for "eyes on." There's also a protective delusion that happens to pilots. When you hear that someone has "bought the farm" (died), the immediate mental Band-Aid is that "It couldn't have happened to me." It sucks for him, but I have luck and skill on my side. Insane thinking, but I swear it's real. How else can you wake up in the morning and strap on your bird (plane), fly hard, and come back to land on a pitching deck of an aircraft carrier at night?

It's hard to describe the next 24 hours. I so wanted to be John Wayne with an "I eat nails for breakfast" look on my face. Instead, I shook. From training habits, I checked that my locator beacon was on, to allow Jolly Green or dustoff helicopters to find and rescue me. I also remembered to collapse my chute, making it more difficult for Charlie to spot and capture me. It was about 1600 hours (4:00 p.m.) and I remember looking around for Charlie. Ben, my GIB, was nowhere to be seen and would be MIA (missing in action). Ben would have been within two miles of me if he was alive. But not a sound, not a flare, nothing. Ultimately, he beams to this day on the Vietnam wall in Washington, D.C. We lost so many in that war and I still don't know why. But in years to follow, when other wars and battles flared, someone always asked me how I felt about them. They expected, "Let's get 'em." But my response was always a very simple single question: "Ever been in a war, friend?" That's your answer.

The temperature was excruciating in Nam and that day was probably no exception. I say "probably" because I was shaking and chilled. Shock. I took my helmet off and put a smoke flare in my hand as I dunked down to neck-high in the rice soup. And now came the fun. Wait and shake. You'd think that I might remember every thought in my head that night as the interminable minutes crawled by, but I couldn't. Home, wife, God, family, childhood? I hadn't a clue. The beauty of shock and panic is their ability to cover you like a warm blanket in winter. But their evil never leaves completely, and erupts without prompts in an evening dream.

In a blink, the night covered me. I do remember how spectacularly the night sky was lighted with stars. I would have preferred that it be filled with a rescue helicopter. No such luck, and I couldn't stop scanning the sky to look for help. It's only now, years later, that I can admit how much I cried that night. Truth be told, I still have occasional private cry nights these many years later. The dream is always the same. I eject but the chute doesn't open so I spread my arms open like wings and try to fly my body into the rice patty. I awake abruptly before my touchdown on the rice pond. My bed is usually soaked in sweat and I always apologize to my wife in the morning. Even my psych-shrink sessions haven't eliminated the episodes. Christ! It's been more than 50 years.

But here's the thing. All during my rice bath in Agent Orange that night, I regressed for a while. I bargained with the Man Upstairs. "Please, God, send help. Send some Green Berets in. Anything. I'll start believing again. I'll put down my Marlboros and Chivas Regal. I swear I'll be good." Throw in a gallon of sobbing real tears and maybe the shaking would stop. God, I was glad no one could see me so broken. My father would have been disgusted.

He would have recommended a lap around the beads (rosary beads). I so wanted to hear the sound of "whop-whop" helicopter blades coming towards me.

This sounds corny, I know, but I swear it's the truth. Sometime in the early morning with the sun starting to rise as my panic was rising, I got pissed. What the hell was I doing here? This sucked, big time.

"Well, screw 'em and the rest of my friends back home having a Schlitz right now. You want me, m----f---ers! Come and get it. I don't need any goddamn helo. I'll walk the hell out of here!" Ain't it great to be young and naïve? Hell, I couldn't walk a yard an hour in the muck I was standing in. It's not as if I could try hitching a ride on Highway 95 back to the carrier.

That's when my grandmother's words came back to me. They made me feel like a true badass. If only the shaking would stop. But the shaking was the real me then and there. Scared and really confused. I'm sure that's why I remember so little of that day. It comes back to me only in pieces during an occasional nightmare. A big "sorry" goes to my wife for the inadvertent kicking and sweat. Even now at age 75 I occasionally dream back to pure panic.

Whop-whop-whop! I was sandbagged in a dustoff Huey helicopter compliments of the Army, heading to Saigon and a full medical evaluation. I did a lot of Marlboros and Chivas that week with time off in Saigon. Sorry, God.

Chapter Two
Grandma's Words

"There's no kindness in the world unless it is first given."
- Unknow

I was probably six years old when I first realized that my life had been formatted to be different from that of most other children I knew and would meet. It wasn't a blockbuster realization, but none of my kindergarten classmates had my life's craziness. Of course, I never knew that my life was crazy until my teen years. But I'm getting a tad ahead of myself.

I know that now in my late aging years, I have a hint of understanding about how a disaster at one moment will pass and that I can only grow or rot from the experience. Some say that tough times either kill you or make you stronger. I've changed it to the idea that tough times can make you stronger if you so choose, but they won't kill you against your will. They only delay the inevitable.

At six, I first recall being at my grandmother's house. Even now, I think of her as the kindest woman I would ever know. So gentle. So caring. I still remember the smell of her tattered flannel bathrobe. She would say each morning, "Come give Grammy a snuggle." She would smother my face in her bathrobe and I could smell the years of bacon and biscuits that she had made each morning. I still love bacon and biscuits. To hell with my cholesterol.

On one particular morning with crisp untouched snow in the yard, I got up and walked into the kitchen. The house was asleep. Most importantly, my mother was still asleep. We were at my grandmother's house in Vermont for Christmas and I loved her cramped fragrant kitchen. Grandma lived on a paltry pension from the Rutland railroad after she retired (was fired). We had a woodstove and my job was to bring in wood from the porch. I still call my food freezer an icebox because that's exactly what it was. Stan the iceman came by daily in his horse-drawn wagon and grabbed a chunk of ice to sling on his back. He wore a leather cape to keep the ice off his back, but to me it was borrowed from Superman. Stan was a big burly guy and he always had something to say to me like, "Stop growing so fast, kiddo," as he handed me a dirt-covered carrot. "Run down and give Dexter a treat." I loved feeding that horse and he grew to know me, shaking his tail as I approached.

Sounds like an idyllic setting, doesn't it? Did I mention that my mother was there? Ellen, as I called her, never Mom, was the enemy. The one to be truly feared. How she could be the daughter of the kindest grandmother ever is beyond me. Maybe Darwin has the answer, but I don't.

On this morning of enlightenment, as I smelled the delicious odors of Grandma's kitchen, my radar eyes spied a box of Entenmann's chocolate doughnuts. Damn, they were high above my reach, but that was never a challenge for a sugar monster. Was I really a sugar monster? You bet. And years later I would realize why. Sugar raises a neurotransmitter in the brain called serotonin.

Yup, the same stuff that antidepressants stimulate. So if you're feeling a little down, you need a serotonin spike. What's better than chocolate doughnuts for a six-year-old? Later in life I learned that cigarettes, booze, carbohydrates, and a host of other wickeds would do the same.

So what does a six-year-old craving hugs and petrified of his mom do? Have a doughnut? No. You never know when your next serotonin spike will be, so eat them all! I became the champion six-year-old doughnut/cookie monster. And this particular day, I managed to wolf down ten of 12. Not bad for a rookie, but talk about pissing off my siblings! We weren't a close-knit Ozzie-and-Harriet family at all. The home situation had engendered an environment of self-survival above everyone else. Brother, sister? Just names of the enemy.

I headed back into my bed feeling a tad sickly and disgustingly full. There should be a Saint Serotonin to pray to for relief. Warm, snug, and wrapped in little-boy dreams, I dreamt of six-year-old bliss. Maybe I dreamt of being locked in a candy store. Who knows?

SPLASH! Freezing cold Vermont water smacked my face, covering my pillow. Good morning to my world. Ellen put the glass down and was now beating the covers with my fanny underneath. Of course, she was so hung over from the night's drink-fest she never realized that the blankets shielded my precious butt. Nevertheless, immediate crying and wailing ensued. I think, at that stage, the tears were more from drama and fear than from pain. All I could hear was shrill screaming from my mother that had no decipherable words for me. One more smack, and she was done.

My grandmother came running in and I imagine her yelling at her daughter to stop. Frankly, I don't remember for sure, but that would have been her loving style. Grandma moved me to the other side of the bed and off the wet sheets. And here's when I first learned that my beliefs about my parents were real, not the fabrications of some wimpy kid. My grandma held and rocked me as I sobbed, and it felt so good. Serotonin on steroids. Then she offered those words that would get me through the worst night of my life. She told me to be strong.

"Your mom isn't well, Tommy. You need to take care of yourself. Can't count on others ever. Be strong. You can do it all, my grandson."

I wish that episode had ended right there, but of course Ellen wasn't through. She needed to teach me how mean a boy I was and how I had ruined her day. I liked that last part. So before breakfast Ellen grabbed me by the hair on the back of my neck and pulled me to the sink. Now, by this time, my brothers and sister were awake and drooling about the biscuits and bacon. Stan had delivered the ice but Dexter would get no carrot from me that day. Over the sink, my mother grabbed the lye soap and pushed it into my mouth. A mushy pepper lollipop. Not even biscuits and bacon would rid me of that taste. It would not be my last taste. Again, Grandma to the rescue, pulling the soap out of Ellen's hand and yelling, "Ellen, Ellen! For God's sake!"

I ran to my room and assumed the familiar fetal position. Grandma brought in a plate of bacon and biscuits, but no more food for me. Only the joy of sleep and being so thankful for my grandmother.

That was an early lesson on how kindness can save, and an unforgettable indelible branding on me to take responsibility for myself.

Chapter Three

Good Ol' Russ and Ellen

There is wisdom in every man, in every father, in your father. And that's true whether you love him or despise him.
- Joe Kita

No such thing as a bad mother, but there sure are very "not well" mothers.
- Me

Just as my mother was "Ellen," so too my father was "Russ," not "Dad." And he definitely was not the patriarch of our family. It was a matriarchal household from the moment we opened our eyes in the morning. Russ was already out of the house catching the New Haven train to Manhattan and Ellen was the warden to deal with all day. Thank God for school.

Russ was a truly brilliant man with a scholarly background of Jesuit prep school, Stevens Institute of Engineering and Columbia University. He was addicted to rockets and aviation and, as a young man, in 1926, went to Auburn, Massachusetts for the first liquid-fuel rocket launch by Robert Goddard. Quite an accomplishment for a bright kid from the Bronx. He left Stevens because they didn't have advanced courses in rocketry. After graduating from Columbia as a Phi Beta Kappa, he joined the Army Air Corps but spent World War II teaching in Carlisle, Pennsylvania, at the Army's War College because he didn't make the weight requirement of 136 pounds to enter flight school. He weighed 126. In an attempt to meet the requirement, he drank banana milkshakes for six weeks and gained a measly two pounds. Devastated, he resigned after the war and went to work for McCann-Erickson, advertising agency.

McCann was the premier advertising company in the world and produced many of the most popular TV shows of the 1950s: *Howdy Doody*, *Gunsmoke*, *The Loretta Young Show*, *The Jimmy Durante Show*, and more. I was an extra on several of those shows as a young boy. Pretty exciting, right? Actually, it sucked. Please remember that I was definitely a stringbean dweeb. I could chat about ancient Greek and Latin, but had no idea who Stan Musial or Babe Ruth were. I was once ordered to be an escort for Hayley Mills, a teenage star of Walt Disney movies. What a great night. I was in a rented tuxedo holding a putrid-smelling corsage for Hayley. It was her "cotillion" at the Waldorf Astoria Hotel in midtown Manhattan. I dutifully awaited her presence at the entrance to the hotel. Debutantes and young studs passed me with an occasional look that said, "What's that dork doing here?" I met Hayley at the stairs with photographers and her other escort from some Connecticut prep school. We entered the ballroom and, get this, that's the last I ever saw of her. I stayed gawking for about an hour and then left and went for a slice of pizza up the street. To my friends who asked what it was like, I said she was all over me and I copped a feel and got some French. To this day, I hope that some of my buds bought the lie, but I doubt it.

Russ felt as if he was still in the Army. He had one goal for me: to be a cadet at West Point. "She walks, she talks, she full of chalk. The lacteal fluid extracted from the female of the bovine species is prolific to the nth degree." That was one of the trivial facts plebes must memorize. How do I recall that 65 years later? No, I was never a plebe, other than in Russ's eyes. I was given a plebe fact every Saturday while listening to the West Point band on the Victrola while standing at attention. I was never allowed to sleep using a pillow because, in Russ's mind, it would curve my back, thus ruining my "attention" posture. Crazy? Just getting started.

Brandy was Russ's drug of choice around the clock. He was truly addicted. Yet drunk or sober, he remained one of the best speakers I've ever heard. I don't know how he could write and lecture so well or even walk with so much Christian Brothers-brand cognac flowing through his veins. Naturally, it had to be "Christian Brothers" cognac for a daily Catholic Mass-goer such as he.

Scrupulous to a fault, he never waivered from his beliefs. Nuts as they were, he followed them to a tee. Unfortunately, he demanded his offspring do the same. Case in point:

My best friend in grammar school was Billy Ruzza. Billy was a great kid from a 100 percent Italian family. His dad was a house painter, but I never saw any paint. I learned years later as an adult that "Willy" Ruzza Senior ran the Mafia in Westchester County, New York. I spent most Sundays at Billy's house where a full-day "mangia" eating fest took place. Anita, Billy's mother, was always stuffing me. Her only fault was yelling at Billy with, "How come you can't be smart like Tommy? Tommy, teach him sumptin'." But

Billy wanted nothing to do with books. For me, they were a respite. I can dream up the taste of Anita's meatballs to this day.

One day after school I went to Billy's house to fool around in his father's barn garage, an amazing haven for a snoop like me. There on a wooden counter was Billy's cap gun. It looked so real. And a box of caps was there; it couldn't get better. I had to have it. Without thinking I hid them in my pants and told Billy I had to go home, hoping he wouldn't see the gun.

Voila, I was home and shooting rolls of caps out of my bedroom windows. Pity the bird or squirrel that entered my gun's sight. Did I say "my" gun? Well, not for long. That night my father saw the used caps on my floor and demanded an answer. I showed him the gun and explained that Billy loaned it to me. My father knew me too well. A quick phone call to the Ruzzas' house and hell was on its way.

My father grabbed me and brought me to our kitchen and put my hand over an already red electric coil for heating pans. He held my hand about an inch over the scorching coil and the heat was unbearable, so I tried to pull my hand away. My right ring finger touched the coils. I was screaming and my father told me this was for lying and stealing. I ran to my room yelling. Again, my brothers and sister could only hide in fear. Would that ever happen to them? No. But 65 years later, I still rub the end of my right ring finger and feel the scar nodule. Makes for a great fingerprint, though. A couple of tumblers of cognac and my dad was relieved enough to grab me by the arm and walk me back to Billy's house with the gun. He coached my very apologetic words to Billy and Anita, who met us at the door. Billy actually felt worse for me than I did.

Yes, Russ could be physical. Once he came up behind me after a few tumblers and wrapped me in his arms from behind. A love hug? No, a reminder to stand up straight. Problem was the squeeze. He actually broke two opposite-sided ribs. Today they continue to protrude. Not a problem, really, but I'll never be good at yoga. Not sure what my mother told the emergency-room doctor. Tough to blame that injury on falling down stairs.

Here was Russ's favorite: Whenever I would screw up, like eating unauthorized cookies, Ellen would use her hairbrush on my bottom, yelling, "Wait 'til your father gets home!" Ah, the famous phrase of the 1950s. And then the dreaded moment came when Russ was home. Some fake tears from Ellen and a quick explanation of the felony, and the family was called to the living room. The family sat around and Russ took a chair to the middle of the room. Off came his belt and down came my pants as I lay over his knees. For me, I was internally yelling in my brain, "Bring it on, bastard." Always a silent internal scream, because saying those words out loud would bring on a godawful retaliation. But I can only imagine the fear that it caused in my brothers and sister. They lived with their self-imposed internal panic that sounded like, "God, don't let that happen to me." One brother, though, was never there. My brother Mark.

Mark was my love. He was completely handicapped. He made Stephen Hawking look like an Olympic runner. He never spoke, never ate on his own, but could understand, laugh, and cry. He rarely cried. My job was to care for him whenever our aide (usually from Scotland or Jamaica), was off duty or had resigned. I truly loved my brother Mark. He would furl his lips for "no" and lower his jaw for "yes." And we spoke volumes with only those responses and tons of laughs. I fed him baby food all of his life, and dis-impacted his rectum every two days. It always took two people to bathe him because he was so spastic. Who helped with the bathing when the aide wasn't around? Russ! Yup, the same guy who wasn't shy with a belt for me loved my brother Mark. Scrupulously religious, Russ thought of Mark as a living saint, a real God-ordained saint. It was amazing. He'd even take Mark for walks in the wheelchair. He always thanked the aides for whatever they were doing. To his credit, Russ never relented in caring for Mark. He never struck any of my siblings either. They never felt any love from him, but suffered no torture other than fear. I guess that counts. On the other hand, Ellen barely knew Mark was alive. Except for family pictures. In those, there she was, holding Mark. What a sad joke.

A little secret from 70 years ago: I never called Mark by his name. I made one up. It was "Umpy." I have no idea where I came up with that, but Umpy was my love. He taught me love, patience, caring, acceptance, and so much more. I am here because of him. Here's something spooky. After marrying Merrill in my fifties, I happened to be traveling one weekend. Merrill went with a girlfriend to a "spiritualist" one evening. Knowing that I would have been laughingly sarcastic at the thought, she didn't tell me where she was going. Nonetheless, off she went, and damn if the gal spiritualist didn't pick her out and ask, "Who is Umpy?" Merrill, shocked beyond belief, explained. Then the spiritualist said, "And what does hepatitis B have to do with you?" Merrill told her that we were adopting our daughter from China and she had hepatitis B. Inexplicable, weird, and just plain spooky. I'm not a believer, but that episode did loosen my tight hold on skepticism. Weird, and put in my box labeled "No freakin' idea how to explain."

Ever wonder if "What goes around comes around" really happens? Well, here's a whopper. Russ was a devout Catholic and a devout anti-Semite. Yes sir, he hated Jews. Not sure why, other than he believed the Jews crucified Jesus. But my neighbor buddy was Kurt Bernstein. We shot hoops in the afternoon. After sweating it up, I'd have Kurt into the house for goodies. When Russ was there, no one could have been more polite. "Oh, hi, Kurt. How are you and how are your parents?" The epitome of courtesy. But when Kurt left it was, "Keep that Jew boy out of here." It never stopped me, and Kurt and I would laugh about it outside. Nuts is nuts. But here's the "swear to God" karma. I flew up to see my father on his deathbed in his then small smoke-filled apartment. He was dying from lung cancer after smoking three packs a day probably since birth. My wife at the time, Diane, criticized me for going on the trip. "He doesn't want you there. He won't let you stay more than 15 minutes after an all-day trip to get there. It's stupid!" But she never understood that I didn't do it for Russ. I did it for me. It was, as a son, my duty. You did what was the right thing to do. Everything else was bull.

But, oh yeah, the karma. While dawdling at Russ's bedside that day in July 1997, as he lay dying, I noticed a massive Bible on his nightstand. It looked like the Oxford dictionary. Bored, I flipped it open to the middle and there before my eyes was a portion of the family tree. I can't even recall how far back it went because it was thrown on the floor after I noticed a name: Julius Bellesheim. "Who's this Julius guy?" I asked. The book hit the floor and Russ yelled, "He's a goddamn Jew and isn't supposed to be in that book!" What the hell?! My great-grand uncle was Jewish! Holy crap. Talk about karma. And a few years ago, my current wife, Merrill, had me do a genetics test. I had long since forgotten about uncle Julius and Russ. But the results showed I was eight percent Ashkenazi Jew. So sorry, Russ, but your son is part Jewish. Be careful whom you hate and why.

There were countless abuses by Russ throughout the years, but the important aspects of his behavior involve the "why," the surviving, and the effects on the family. "Why" is simple. It was his only way of coping with feelings of insecurity and having to deal with a crazy wife who he felt strongly was going to hell, and the guilt of having brought my brother Mark into this world. Lash out, drink, work incessantly, love and pity my brother Mark, pay no attention to the others, and enjoy depression. But he needed a target. My brothers and sister cowered. Not good targets for a military man. Tom? Perfect. Tom was always getting in trouble and handled all beatings with a "can't touch me" attitude. He probably thought his beatings didn't affect me. And here's the thing: They could have affected me by directing me down one of two roads. One road was to copycat his and Ellen's behavior in my own life. The other road was "Screw you. I can do this job of living better, saner, and kinder than the both of you." I chose the latter path, but honestly I have no idea why. Put me on the quiz show *Jeopardy* and the answer I'd choose would be "Mark, my brother, for a thousand, Alex."

But how do you survive? I'm sure many don't, particularly when you look at the history of child abusers today. Almost all were abused. What's good for the goose is good for the gander. My sadness, hate, and depression triggered a response in me. I swore that my own children would never know such a life. I could do it. How could any parents act so insanely? I remember swearing to myself over and over again that I would not. And I could openly defy and continually bust my parents' brains on a daily basis. Some will say that I deserved what I got. Maybe so, had I been in a prison. And for years I had to deal with that conundrum. But with time I learned that no child deserves lack of love and beatings. Not one. As a kid you can make it without a bike, or, in today's parlance, an iPhone, but you can't make it without kindness.

So I must hate my Russ. No, I don't at all. Pity? Yes. But for all that happened at the hands of my father, I am who I am today because of him, Ellen, and Mark. The cost to me was surely anger, and it probably played a major role in my choice for combat flying in Vietnam. And yes, I still work on anger. Blatant unkindness in others makes me wish I had a fighter jet with 2.75 rockets locked and loaded. Sorry. I'm working on it. And my mantra when remembering Russ's actions? "That's the best that he could do." I wish that I could take credit for that mantra, but it came to me ten years ago. My anger and depression had internally fermented. No one saw it in me because it had been ingrained in me not to show "weakness." I confided these feelings gently to my daughter Kristy. She is a physician certified in family medicine and psychiatry. She suggested that I meet with Dr. Geoffrey Sternlieb in San Diego. Geoff was brilliant with me and we have become great friends. I remember him asking how angry I was with my brother Mark. I swore to him that I loved Mark and he taught me so much. Geoff kept pushing. "Why no anger when cleaning his rectum or being laughed at by the other kids when wheeling Mark?" I spat back at Geoff, "Because that's the best he could do, goddamn it." There was a long pause and then he sucker-punched me by asking about Ellen and Russ. Did I learn from them? Was it the best they could do? Okay, okay, Perry

Mason, I get it. And that phrase has fueled my breath more times than I can say. It acts like a fire hose on my flame of anger.

And then there's Ellen. A book in herself, she's almost indescribable. But I'll give it a shot. First, she was overwhelmed. Five kids with one totally handicapped. What do you do? Hide and put blinders on. Medication? Sure, gin and valium make for a comfortable world, but not a comfortable one for your children. Ellen decided that safe hiding started with avoiding my brother Mark. She had virtually nothing to do with him. But he was always good for an excuse. A speeding ticket: "I'm so sorry, Officer, but I have a cerebral palsy child at home and just heard he's choking!" New tires for her car? "I have a dying cerebral palsy child at home that I take to the hospital in my car. What can I get as a deal? I'll notify United Cerebral Palsy and have them call your discount a donation." Constantly looking for sympathy. Daily. And yet she barely knew Mark. To this day, her behavior to him makes me want to vomit. My takeaway to this day is revulsion when I see or hear of unkind behavior. Unfortunately, it truly was the best that she could do.

Ellen had other tricks she liked. Lots of her day was spent in bed watching "soaps." *As the World Turns* was a favorite. It's hard to write about some of her craziness, but it's important to know how egregious the family environment was to live in. So bad that at 16 I ran away. Of course, I was too young to realize how evil some of her actions to me were, but they surely were. Her afternoons would find her lying in bed with her gin and tonic, calling for me to sit on her bed and talk about the day at school. While I described my day, she took a bottle of baby oil, spread her legs, and massaged her genitals. Then she guided my hand and had me do it. For years I felt as if this was simply another task for the oldest son. Not sure I've ever gotten over that. I have a reminder that I see in the mirror each morning: a scar over my right eyebrow. For some long-forgotten reason, I must have said something that pushed her buttons and she grabbed a Pond's Cold Cream jar to hit me. I never saw it coming before its impact over my eye. Blood was suddenly everywhere. A towel for direct compression while Ellen dressed, and off to the emergency room and another report to the doctor of a clumsy kid running into the corner of a door. In those days, child abuse was not reportable. It was life in the 1950s.

In later years, I had a more formal course in sex from Rose, one of Mark's aides, living with us in the bedroom next door from mine. She started innocently by bringing me into her room and teaching me to smoke. Many coughs later, I became a walking chimney that lasted through my days in Vietnam. Gradually she became an anatomy professor. She not only enjoyed her own body but was an equal opportunity employer and enjoyed mine as well. Not that as a 12-year-old I had much sexual expertise. But Rose was very kind and good with Mark. She was lonely and playful. I had my first taste of beer with Rose. I guess she was a version of a Cliff's Notes book about the facts of life never otherwise taught to a young lad. She didn't have an evil bone in her body and was a great confidante. She knew all too well the pathology of Ellen and Russ. That was a great relief for a boy hating his parents and questioning his own sanity. That, I had been taught, was against the law of God. Any support was an incredible relief. As soon as Rose found a boyfriend, older than 12 and needing no teaching, she was gone. End of story, with no follow-up.

But back to Ellen. Did you ever take a walk on concrete or near a stone wall? Of course you have. And have you noticed a small green plant or flower growing out of a crack? How can that happen? It makes no sense. Well, that's how I remember Ellen. On the wall that she was in my life, there was one amazing tiny flower that stood out. When I was 13, Ellen and Russ decided that my evil ways needed a religious scrubbing. As religious fanatics, they had numerous priests as friends. It was not unusual to have one or two priests as dinner guests and even a Mass in our living room. So Father Pat Collins felt that a weekend retreat in Gloucester, Massachusetts, would be miraculous. You weren't far off, Father Pat, but it sure wasn't what I had been taught was miraculous.

Ellen, Russ and I drove to Gloucester to a Jesuit retreat house. A retreat, by the way, is a silent time of prayer and religious teaching in order to fire up your religious fervor. But this special retreat surely backfired. Ellen and Russ kept reminding me of how blessed I was to have my own private retreat. I'm reminded of that every time someone tells me to "have a blessed day." No, thank you.

We arrived at dinner and Father Pat had it all ready for us in the kitchen. After dinner there was prayer and a sermon. In a retreat house, everyone has their own room. Extremely stark. Hard bed, desk, and light. No television or radio. No bathroom. The shower and bathroom were communal and down the hall. Don't even imagine it came close to a comfortable room at Motel 6. But after a long drive from New York in a smoke-filled car, then dinner and prayer, I was ready for bed.

Shortly after I had drifted off to the smell of sacred candles, I was gently awakened by Father Pat, who wanted to chat some more with me. Ellen and Russ were sound asleep. So, dutifully, I followed Father Pat to his study. It was quite sumptuous. Leather chairs, fireplace, and wall-to-wall books. There was the telltale smell of cigarettes and brandy, well known to me. Please understand, priests were actually God to me. I had been raised to believe that, and, in fact, thought them to be the word and hand of God. That night I learned that this priest was the word of Satan incarnate. He sat in a large leather chair and while telling me that I was a very good boy and how proud he was of me, he beckoned me to him. He sipped gingerly on his brandy and offered me a sip. I politely declined but he insisted, and you don't deny God's representative. Some gentle petting progressed to undoing my sash pajama belt and dropping the pants to my ankles. Next came my white jockey underpants, and, well, you know the rest, I'm sure. I remember crying and pulling up my pants and running out of the study after a minute or so. How big of a mortal sin had I just committed? How could godlike Father Pat do that! Christ! Where the hell was Christ when I needed him most?

So here's that flower in the wall. Screaming, I ran back to my room. It was adjacent to Ellen's and Russ's room. Ellen ran out of her room sober as a judge and Russ was right next to her in a flash. Sobbing, I spurted out what Father Pat had done. My next recall was of the floor. Russ smacked me across my neck, missing my face. He started calling me a lying bastard and that I was heading to hell. He wanted me to apologize to the satanic man. And here's the kicker. To this day, I have no idea why or how this flower in the wall sprouted. But Ellen grabbed my arm and pulled me up, saying "Shut up, Russ! We're leaving." Bags packed and out the door we went. It must have been close to midnight, but "Mom" was in control. Russ never drove or had a license, so he had no choice. We never spoke about the incident again but it did not put a dent in Russ's religious passion. I bet he even went to Mass for Father

Pat. I doubt my name was ever mentioned. No sense going to hell for having a devil for a son. I was in high school at the time and within a few days, the headmaster, a Jesuit priest, called me into his office to give me a blessing and confirm to me that I had done nothing wrong. It would be years before the abuse scandal in the Church became public. When it did, I was in my fifties and my wife, Merrill, suggested I write to the provincial (the head of the New England Jesuits). I wrote about the experience only to help support other claims, asking for no compensation, and Father Pat was probably dead so no punishment for him. What a kind and pleasant letter I received in return. Oh, no. I never heard a word from the provincial. A lawyer friend explained that had they replied in any way, it would be an admission of guilt. The eleventh commandment: "Cover your butt!"

So how do you look back and have any of that make sense? I don't have the best answer, but I do have some ideas that ease the anger. First, I absolutely believe that it was the best they could do. Why? Because everyone involved had solid pathology. Diagnoses such as psychopath, bipolar, sociopath, or personality disorder I would study in medical school years later. But do labels truly matter? Not to me. Some will criticize that as naïve on my part. Perhaps so. But it lets me sleep at night.

I learned to breathe in the lyrics of a song: "In the end, only kindness matters." I can take all of the healthy superlatives and qualities we all strive for (work ethic, love, honesty, and so on) and they lose all their backbone without kindness. Not always an easy task for me but it's a struggle that is worth it. Tough to buy? Participate in a war and you can't come away with any thought other than "Where in the hell is kindness?"

Much to learn from and much to avoid in my own life, but I love this analogy. I recall this story because I remember it daily. Once there was an elderly monk who took his young student to the river to sit. The old monk noticed a drowning scorpion in the river struggling to stay alive by grasping a twig. The old monk reached down to rescue the scorpion but the young student grabbed his arm and said, "No, Master, he will bite and kill you." The old monk continued scooping the scorpion and placing him on dry ground. As he let him go, the scorpion bit him and the monk began to die on the riverbank. The young student exclaimed, "Why, Master?" The old monk looked at him and said, "The scorpion did what is in his nature. I chose my nature and did the same."

Please don't get me wrong. I'm not looking for scorpions or rattlesnakes. But I've dealt with similar types of people. I now know that they're going to do what is in their nature and their own best interests. Nothing I can do about it. What I can do is the right thing. Search, study, evaluate to find the right, fair, and kind action and then pull a Nike: Do It! Hey, come to think about it, that makes me kind of a saint. Hah! Not even close. My behavior has been nothing less than selfish from that first slap on the bottom back in Carlisle, Pennsylvania. And the world knows that many have been hurt by my actions in a heartless war. You can't come out of a war and feel good about yourself unless you're delusional. And some need the delusion in order to live with themselves.

It's important to know that we all do things to survive depending on the "war" you find yourself in. Ellen and Russ ran a jungle combat war 24/7. Without doubt, surviving that war left you in one of three camps. You became excruciatingly angry, blindly selfish, or miserably fearful. I traveled from camp to camp but spent almost no time in "fearful." I don't know why that was, honestly, except that anger took over and was constant. Whether it was Ellen bursting into my fourth-grade class in her nightgown and curlers to pull me out by my ear to come home and make my bed or to dump a garbage pail over me in my bed, war was always on. But how angry can a 12-year-old get? I truly wanted to survive, and that meant needing Ellen and Russ dead. Really? For sure. So I woke up early one morning and took all of my parents' drinking cups down from the shelf and sprayed them with Raid insect killer. I sprayed the inside of their old coffeemaker, the type with the glass top that showed it percolating. It didn't work, but it did give them a nasty first sip of coffee in the morning! It also got me another reminder of my obstetrician's smack. It wasn't until years later in a shrink's office that Dr. Geoff Sternlieb suggested it was more than a silly prank. Okay, Doc, maybe I'll admit that I was a tad angry.

We can't leave my brother Mark without delving into his effect on the family. It was profound. For any family that has or is managing a disabled child in their home, the parental strain is obvious. What is not as clear is the stress and conflict for other siblings. Imagine if you are a healthy sibling in a family with a disabled child and somehow must deal with horrendous emotions. How do you deal with realizing that your disabled brother or sister is getting tons of attention and sympathy from a nanny while you remain a wallflower? Your parents might not be able to attend your sports or hobby events because of their time with your disabled sibling. And if that spurs some anger or jealousy on your part, how rotten a bastard must you be to have those feelings? In my case, I was angriest at other kids. When I walked Mark in his wheelchair, kids would always run up yelling, "What's wrong with him?" "Does he talk?

Does he walk? Why does he look so funny?" I'd be lying if I said that taunts like that didn't embarrass me when I was young, but, again, it stoked up the fire of anger. Who the hell did they think they were? The dirtbags. Where were manners, decency, and kindness? Not in my neighborhood. But it wasn't all grief. On Saturday mornings, for example, my other brother Ruddy and I would take Mark into the TV room. Every Saturday there was a religious show starring Oral Roberts, and Oral would call disabled people down to his stage. He would shake them and pray over them. Some dropped their crutches or fainted. Quite a show. Rudd and I held Mark up to the screen and pressed his face to it and yelled, "Heal! Heal!" over and over again. Mark would laugh hysterically and always peed in his diaper. Rudd and I then argued over who was going to change the diaper. Mark actually understood everything. He could respond only with facial grimaces meaning yes or no, but he absolutely understood everything. More importantly, he taught us to love and understand kindness. He spoke more to me than anyone ever would in my life.

Mark was thrilled by any and all attention and, as mentioned, Ellen couldn't deal with him. Hence, various aides came and went in our house like bullets out of a 50-caliber machine gun. And then there was Myrtle. Actually, I thought of her as "Saint" Myrtle. Not only was she an amazing relief for me, but her name was spelled "k-i-n-d-n-e-s-s." Myrtle was from Jamaica. She came to the States for refuge and Catholic Charities managed her until she found us. She moved into a small room next to Mark and was solidly happy. Most importantly, she fell madly in love with Mark. With her Catholic background, she saw Mark as a gift from God and a blessing to all who came in contact with him. Her day off? She stayed with Mark and seldom cared for herself. How she was able to handle

Ellen and Russ was theater to be seen. Ellen would yell at her, Russ never would, and Myrtle would become a turtle. She went silent and retreated to her room. I heard her praying in there once and can't imagine how she'd pray for Ellen. Oh yeah, Saint Myrtle.

Mark influenced all members of the family. Sissie, the eldest and only female of the kids, had a very hard time with Mark. It might have been all of the medical dealings with Mark that threw her. Years later she could never go to a doctor's office without a tranquilizer. She would always faint whenever blood had to be drawn. She'd vomit just hearing the word "blood." She never married and, of course, never had children. Sissie lived in her own world. She ended up teaching fourth grade for 40 years. And truth be told, she was a great teacher and loved by her students. Thank God none of them ever had any bleeding.

Myrtle stayed with Mark for the rest of his life. I'm getting ahead of myself, but before I ran from the Ellen-Russ cauldron for survival, they sent Mark to the Kennedy home in Rhode Island. Rose Kennedy, yes, of the famous Kennedy family, set it up for severely handicapped children. Mark died there in 1968 from "untreated" pneumonia. In those days, if severely handicapped children contracted an infectious disease, the disease was left to take its course. Myrtle moved to the Kennedy home and lived with Mark. She was there on the day he died. Sadly, we couldn't locate Sissie to notify her and so she did not attend his funeral. She had "left home" as I had, but we didn't know where she was staying. Myrtle is buried next to Mark and nothing could be more fitting.

Russ was truly hit hard when Mark died, and the alcohol intake increased. He really had little in his life without Mark. He was an inveterate reader and that's about it. His interest was focused on my academics, particularly while I was in grammar school. His favorite time was when the report cards from school came home. He would give me a dollar for every 100 percent that I received. A 98 percent got me the ridicule of "Slug, it wouldn't have taken any more effort to get a hundred percent." He loved perfection in my work but never my siblings'. I still can't figure out why. But it taught me, so that I have never looked at a single report card from my children. I'd simply ask, "How do you like how you did?" "What's your game plan to improve?" All three children are sane and very bright. No dollars were ever given to them by me.

I can't look back on the childhoods of my brothers and sister without more than a tad of sadness. They had to watch beatings and yellings daily, living with the fear that it might one day be them. Living with that kind of fear and stress is like a beaver gnawing on a redwood tree. Sooner or later there will be the well-known cry of "Timber." All of them heard that cry at one time or another. None of them were ever beaten or abused. I asked Sissie once how she dealt with the chaos at home. She was in her sixties at the time. She replied that she didn't recall anything. None of the drinking, beatings, or abuse on me. Unbelievable! Denial truly is a panacea for pain. All of the feelings of fear were gone for her.

Sissie was the eldest and most aloof. Russ had no idea how to handle her so he stayed away from her. Ellen saw her as a kindred female spirit and so they had no real conflicts until the teen years. Then there was screaming at each other but nothing physical. Ellen taught Sissie to drive and so they bonded with four wheels. Russ never drove and never had a license. That drove (no pun intended) Ellen wild. She was the absolute matriarch of the family and so, when Russ was in his late forties, she demanded that he learn to drive. She hired an instructor for him and after Russ complied, he took the test and they mailed him his license. We should have had bumper stickers saying, "My dad is an honor student at driving school." I didn't have a license so all I could do was drool. And here's the thing: Russ never got behind the wheel of a car again. He threw his license away. I smelled tension on the home front. What's new about that?!

Ruddy had loud "Timber!" raging in his ears. The story goes like this. I had left home and was living in the Bronx and occasionally in the garage of a family from a country club that I worked at. I was a caddy and swim teacher/lifeguard. A super-swank country club and Mrs. Appleby, hearing my tales about my home, let me stay in their upstairs garage. Sometimes I stayed in the Bronx with Gene Cotes. Gene was a "hood" (bad kid) in school with me, but that's another story.

Anyway, I would sneak back to the family home and steal money, cigarettes, or any other needs. On one particular night, I slinked in while everyone slept. When I went into my old room that I shared with Rudd, I looked at his bed in the dark. I saw what looked like the Shroud of Turin: a white sheet with a dark body outline in the center. I walked over and touched the sheet to find it soaked. A light on showed my shaking brother covered in blood. He had cut himself with a Gillette blade. He was 13 years old. I don't know which one of us was more petrified. I think I remember him asking me not to say anything.

I ran downstairs to the phone and dialed "0." There was no "911 for emergencies" back then. The police arrived with sirens blaring at 11:00 or 12:00 at night. I opened the door and bleated out what I had seen. By this time, Ellen and Russ were coming down the stairs, Russ in boxers and Ellen in a sheer gown. Quite a sight for the cops. Russ smacked me and explained to the cops that I was a liar and not even living there, and everything was fine. One of the officers didn't buy it. "It won't hurt to check," he said.

Rudd ended up in an ambulance to the New Rochelle hospital and subsequently spent two years at Columbia's psychiatric hospital in New York City. And get this: Only two visitors were allowed. A Jesuit priest from his prep school, and me. Ultimately he did well. He spent most of his time memorizing the Oxford dictionary. When he wrote to me, I couldn't understand half of the words. I think he liked it that way. Interestingly, Rudd had only one hobby. Yup, memorizing words from the dictionary! No need for high SAT scores to figure that one out. Ruddy finished college, a masters' degree, and almost completed a Ph.D. Now married and the father of two, he still has the vocabulary of a *Jeopardy* winner and a great sense of humor. He's a hero to me.

Jon was the caboose of the family. I didn't get to know him well and I regret that to this day. By the time he was 12, I was in the military and had been out of the house since I was 16. So Jon missed most of the craziness with the exception of seeing a few of my beltings when he was a toddler. But he knew about the family insanity. He listened to the alcoholic rants between Ellen and Russ. What'd he do? He carved a door in the back of the closet in his room. It led to an eave under the house roof. Some floorboards and a light: Voila! A mini Garden Hilton! And there he lived out his childhood days. He was a very gifted kid. He took things apart and figured out how to fix damned near everything. His love was his dog. He saved and bought a dachshund he named Blitz. He learned all he could about animals and committed to become a veterinarian. He took courses at Fordham University while still at Fordham Prep. His courses were all superfluous. One of his courses was advanced calculus. Hell, I'm proud just to be able to spell it. Then, before graduation, the college professor died. The dean of the college gave the students options. Take a grade of "withdraw passing," or repeat the course tuition-free next semester. Jon took the withdraw-passing. A week before graduation from prep school, the headmaster, Father Eugene O'Brien, informed him that he would not be graduating until he re-took the calculus in summer school. Now, Jon didn't need the course, had already taken high-school calculus, and had 125 high-school credits when students needed only 90 to graduate. Makes no sense, right? Then why? You'll have to wait to hear about my fiasco of graduating before Jon. But Jon merely transferred to the local public high school, and without setting foot in a classroom was granted a diploma. He was one of the few students in that public school going on to college, and the principal was delighted to have Jon as a graduate. Did it hurt Jon? Who knows? He never pursued veterinary medicine and no one knows why. He finished college and went to work for a little company called McCann-Erickson, the world's largest advertising company. By the way, Russ left McCann as its president! Go figure. Jon prospered and married one of the kindest women I've ever known. Rose remains a love. Jon had an infectious laugh and dry sense of humor. Most might say after meeting him that he was direct and calculating. But what I remember was the day I stopped by to say goodbye before leaving for Vietnam. I had not been around except for brief "Hi"s. Yet there was my youngest aloof brother crying his eyes out. I don't think he knew much about the war, but he clearly knew about me. He dove into an all-encompassing hug while sobbing that I was going off to war. Later in life, Jon buried himself in business and sailing. No children, so both he and Rose traveled whenever they could. One Sunday morning at their summer home on Long Island, Jon was resting on the living-room sofa reading *The New York Times*. He looked up at Rose, smiled, and that was the last thing he did. It was March 2009. He was 49 years old. Ruddy and I gave the eulogy to a packed New York cathedral audience. He was truly loved by his partners throughout the world. Close family? Sissie couldn't attend the funeral because of a vacation that she had planned. Really? Yup.

Every moment we are breathing counts.

Chapter Four

Low School

Challenges are neither good nor bad. They're opportunities.

Grammar school had been an oasis for me. A place away from home. I was at the top of the class academically and what could be better? Lots. Ellen and Russ expected excellence from me. I'm not sure why my siblings got a pass on that score, but whatever they did was fine with an occasional, "I think you can do better if you really try." The difference for me was that doing well academically left me tons of time for reading. Reading was my morphine. I became the book. Not surprisingly, I loved novels about young boys who ran away on tramp steamers or ended up on a ranch working cattle. Whatever happened, it was happening to me. I still love books to the point where my Kindle reader can't hold any more. And after reading, there was always mischief. I think I enjoyed thinking the trouble up more than doing it. Oh, hell, the doing was fun too. Once I conned Billy Ruzza into collecting "lightning bugs" at night. We caught at least a hundred and kept them in a mayonnaise jar. That's not too exciting for two young punks, so I took Billy to the movies next day for 25 cents each. No idea what the movie was, but we could not care less. We were there to attack. Midway through the flick, out came the mayonnaise jar, and from the balcony a hundred lightning bugs found freedom. Billy and I were out the door, footloose and fancy free.

Not all of my pranks went that smoothly. For example, I had a great set of Lone Ranger binoculars, very cool in those days, bought with money I had saved from delivering newspapers. Knowing everyone would want to try them, I decided to coat the black eyecups with shoe polish. Ingenious at 13 years of age, if I do say so myself. Unfortunately, my first victim was unintentional. Billy Ruzza. Billy was everything you'd want in a friend. But he was way overweight and therefore very insecure. He saw the binocs around my neck and immediately grabbed them. I know that I should have stopped him, but I was 13. To the grabber beware. They worked like a charm. Billy looked as if he had whopper black eyes. It was not a school day or there would have been hell to pay. Remember, his dad ran the local Mafia. Evidently, when he got home, Anita, his mom, told him what he looked like and of course he immediately tried to wipe the shoe polish off. Bad move, Waldo! The smearing made a mess and generated a call to Ellen from Anita. I don't blame her. It probably ruined some towels, but Anita did know what price I would pay. Another brush job, but what really hurt was losing my binocs. To this day, I have top-notch binoculars. I practically never use them. I don't have to because all that matters is that I have them sans shoe polish.

I took another hit departing Catholic grammar school. The nuns loved me for only one reason: I was the valedictorian. On the other hand, I totally sucked at every sport. Add that to the fact that every "cool" guy and girl in my class thought of me as a Class A dweeb dork. The other phrase for me was "gay faggot." But in those days, that phrase only meant a wimp. It had nothing to do with sexual preference. But obviously I didn't fit in, except with Billy. And not because I did his homework for him. We were true buds.

It was time to say goodbye with a bang. So I bought a bottle of invisible ink from the local magic shop. We all used Script or Sheaffer pens which used bottled blue ink. Invisible ink came in a similar bottle and was labeled Sipto ink. It came with a fake pen that you drew the ink up into and then you squirted it on someone's white shirt. Man, did it look bad. But in about two to three minutes it oxidized and left only a water spot. What a great invention for someone like me. Even after people knew the gag, it always caused a momentary panic. My idea was to make the panic last longer. I thought that adding real ink to it would prolong the effect. I was a genius without any chemistry classes to my credit!

Each classroom had a holy-water font as you entered. You were expected to dip a finger into it and make the sign of the cross by touching forehead, chest, left shoulder and right. Perfect. I poured my brew into the holy water fonts in each classroom before classes began. I ran out of the cocktail in Classroom 4.

The students piled in at the sound of the bell and the crosses began. Of course, the blue dots on the students' white shirts and blouses weren't fading. Real ink, even diluted with magic invisible ink, doesn't fade: it stains. Duh! Our nun went crazy and I was in panic mode. She didn't even ask, "Who did this?" But like a goober I wanted to allay her panic, so I yelled that it was invisible and would vanish soon. Soon never came. But the hairbrush came quickly. Sister Mary Angela had no choice but to call Ellen. I cleaned erasers and chalkboards for the remaining four months after school until graduation. Hey, if life ain't fun, it ain't worth living, for me.

You might think that being valedictorian would be great. You'd be wrong. Now I was hailed and proclaimed the king of weirdo geeks. But it also meant that I had to apply to a Jesuit prep school in Manhattan. It accepted 100 super geeks from schools in New York. Extraordinary curriculum and 100 percent of its graduates went on to big-league colleges. The prep school was tuition-free, all-male, and in New York City. Just what I needed: a school of eggheads! No, sir! But I took the exam and the letter of acceptance arrived. I promptly tore it up and told my despondent parents that I didn't make the cut. Like all things, it didn't end there. They contacted their Jesuit priest friend who arranged to get me into a similar school in Fairfield, Connecticut. It was an hour away by train both ways, and off I went, back and forth every day with my parents' admonitions to excel because Father Pat had bent over backwards to get me in. Little did they know that one year later at the retreat house, he would want me to bend back frontwards!

Some would guess that my Catholic upbringing was a burden, but it's important to know what a comfort it was for me. In a house of chaos and violence, the Church was a mind spa for me. I desperately needed something to believe in and the Church and altar boys filled that spot. Father McHale was the diocesan priest in charge of the altar boys, or acolytes as we were called. He ran the group like the military. We had our own cassocks (gowns) and starched collars with colored bows for them, depending on the type of Mass being performed. The more services you served at, the more points you'd get. Enough points and you'd sit before McHale for testing of your Latin pronunciation and liturgical understanding. Doing well would earn you a rank patch for your cassock, and the head acolyte wore a small dove on his sleeve. Yes, I desperately wanted to earn the dove.

I spent most of my free time serving at Masses, weddings, and funerals, amassing (yes, pun) tons of points. It was tantamount to being the top Tupperware salesman in the country. And then it happened: The first ding in my religious cloak of comfort.

I was finishing a High Mass (very formal) on Sunday for the monsignor (the head priest in the parish). Monsignor Kiernan was a drunk Friar Tuck, an arrogant man who felt very entitled to his position and the wine that went with it. Mass ended and I was de-vesting him when I smelled the excess wine and saw the staggering gait. No idea what made me say it, but before I could inhale the words back, I blurted, "Monsignor, how much wine can a priest take at Mass before it's a sin?" I have no memory of his words, but I'm sure they weren't "Bless you, my son." I do recall his angry hands on my shoulder as he pushed me out of the sacristy saying something like, "and never come back."

We all have heartaches in life. We all feel dejected. But please understand that being an acolyte was my thread-like hold on all that was good in my life. All that was comfort and all that meant God was wrapped up in being an acolyte, and in a misplaced breath it was gone. Russ got a call from Father McHale that the monsignor wanted me expelled from the school and out of the group of altar boys. Father McHale would speak to the monsignor and, if I stayed home from school for a few days, that would suffice. But I would have to accept expulsion from the group of altar boys. I honestly sobbed in my room for days. I read books about boys who ran away and went on tramp steamers. I never even felt my father's whipping. To this day, I feel every bit of anger towards those three men. I can't be sure if this was a sentinel fissure in my religious faith, but it certainly demoted my God down to "god."

Fairfield Prep was a blowout from day one. A mandatory prep uniform and tons of classical homework. Greek and Latin didn't ruffle my feathers. But I did meet a senior on the train who taught me the cool way to smoke cigarettes. Great. I'd be combat-ready for Vietnam.

Aside from my stellar stupidity in the classics, that probably wouldn't have gotten me kicked out of the Prep. But here's what did. Brian, my senior buddy on the New Haven train up to school each day had great genius ideas. His name should have been Bernie Madoff. He told me that I was a loser for studying Greek and Latin. I got the "loser" part, but what else could you do but struggle with Caesar and Sophocles? Answer from Brian: a "trot." A trot, for those uneducated in crime, was a perfect English translation of the classics. No, no sweat. He didn't have to tell me twice. I was off to a used-bookstore in a New York second. (The only Amazon I knew was somewhere in South America.) Now with trot in hand, bring on *The Aeneid*! I went into my second semester armed and ready for a grade of "A." I copied the chapter for the exam on index cards and my wrist. I was ready for bear. Exam scores came out but there was no grade next to my name. A message came to see Father Sweeney immediately. He confronted me with the fact that I would have received an "A" on the exam because my translation was flawless. In fact, it was as good as his own. His own! Yes, the one he published that became the same damned trot that I had purchased! What freaking luck! Had I used a trot? "Yes, Father." "Thank you for your honesty. Here is your grade of 'F'." I figured at that point there was no grade for honesty. I would later learn that honesty is its own reward but such a rare commodity to find. There must be a gigantic box full of unused honesty awards, probably hidden in hell.

That episode alone, along with my other sub-Mensa-level grades, told me that I was not long for the continued train rides to the Prep. So why not go out with a literal "bang"? I had always loved firecrackers because they were against the law and loud. Someone had told me that cherry bombs were waterproof. Ingenious. I bought a few from Brian and took one to the upstairs bathroom of the Prep building. Lit one and flushed it down the toilet. Kaboom. It blew open a pipe in the junior-year classroom one floor below. It would have been perfect, but nothing in my life had gone smoothly so far, so why start now? Peter Toole, I still remember his name, would forever be Peter Stooley to me. He was in the bathroom at the time, saw the deed, and laughed gleefully. But the little shit turned me in. Bye-bye, Tommy. Quite a thrill for Ellen and Russ and quite a plumbing bill. Damn, they must have been so proud of me! And the take-home message is this: Cherry bombs work underwater.

Anybody care what happens next? After a few more spins with the belt, I was pretty well set to leave home, but smart enough to know I didn't have enough smarts or money to live on my own. Russ was hell-bent on me finishing in a Jesuit prep school. So who better to ask for help than good old Father Pat? Pat had connections at Fordham Prep in the Bronx. A rough neighborhood, but an academically superb school. Russ's father had gone to school there, Russ went there, Russ's brother went there. Christ! A family legacy. The very thought made me puke. But in no time I was a sophomore at the family bastion of academics. Just one prerequisite: Because of my prior astral dynamite record, I would need a retreat with Father

Pat in Gloucester, Massachusetts. I mean, seriously, what could go wrong with that?! And after my third week at Fordham, Ellen, Russ, and I headed for the home of Jesuits and young boys to find Jesus.

You know the details, but prior to that I really thought that my only way to escape to sanity would be to join the priesthood. God was as real to me as Superman. I remember when I learned the truth about Santa Claus I was truly crushed. Crying and all. Hell, that was child's play. This was real life. Suddenly priests and god had feet of clay and they didn't look good. And yes, Ellen did get a weed-growing-in-the-cement-sidewalk Mother award for her behavior when Father Pat sexually accosted me. It wasn't life-changing. Father Pat, however, was clearly a massive influence on my view of authority and religion. My reverence for the Bible was decaying rapidly.

I was then spending as much time as possible away from home. Any lie would do: detention, swim team, tennis, and I'd make stuff up, like cleaning the school chapel. I didn't even know where the chapel was on campus.

The summer before junior year was spent at Montauk, Long Island. Russ was teaching advertising on the island and the family was there as well. I had a job teaching sailing to kids at a local marina. Russ still never drove a car, but Ellen had the company car. It was a T-Bird. Powder blue. What a beauty. And of course, it would look even better with me in it. I just didn't have a license. I mean, seriously, who would put a motor vehicle in the hands of a teenage lunatic? Oh, that's right, it's done every day, even today. Not so for Ellen and Russ. No license for Tommy. Should that stop a lunatic? Not a chance.

One afternoon, Ellen and Russ were gone and the T-Bird was drooling for a spin, or was it me who was drooling? Hard for me to remember. After weighing the pros and cons, the blue Bird and I were cruising down the Montauk highway. Was I thinking about girls or school? Nope. "How fast can this baby fly?" A question that itched to be answered. The answer: 118 miles per hour. Gotta love that baby-blue Bird! Only one thing went awry with the moment. I screamed past the Coast Guard station on the island. I kept driving to the end of the island but at a sane speed after I realized that the Coast Guard Shore Patrol had seen me flying by. I remember pulling over and smoking a Marlboro. Must be safe to return after one butt smoked. On my way back, in the middle of the road at the Coast Guard station was Officer Mooney sitting in wait for Tommy boy. I pulled over and was brought into the Coast Guard station brig (jail), and Officer Mooney called Russ. I have no idea what was said, but I remember Mooney coming in and saying something like, "Looks like we get to keep you as our guest for the night." Yup, Russ thought jail would serve as a decent teacher for me. Let's see if it was! The next morning, Ellen picked me up and told me I would be seeing a judge in the Bronx to hear my legal fate. The judge was actually a nice fellow, babbling about how we all make mistakes and that it was important to learn from them. Now I would not be able to apply for a driver's license until I became 21 years of age. Not to worry, because a license to me was simply an unnecessary appurtenance. To quote the infamous Lone Ranger, "We'll ride again, Tonto." Call me the teenage Lone Ranger.

Unless you're in the turmoil, I'm not sure if anyone can imagine the daily fear and anger fermenting in my gut. I felt as if I were in a washing machine on the spin cycle. Then along came Gene

Cotes. Gene was at the Prep with me. Academically, he was gifted. Emotionally, he was insane. He made me feel relatively stable. He smoked, did drugs, and was good with a knife. Most importantly, he lived in an apartment in the Bronx with his older brother. These were the tenements you'd see if you rode the train into Manhattan. Gene's brother was absent most of the time. God knows what he was doing, but it sure wasn't nuclear research. He was, plainly and simply, a thug. Good news for me was that I could leave school with Gene and stay in the apartment. It turned out that this, too, would be another survival course. I learned the basics of economics. It doesn't take a whiz kid to learn that you need food to eat and it costs money. Cigarettes, beer, wine, and even underpants cost money. Where do you get it? I hadn't a clue. But Gene was as good as a financial planner for ideas and methods on grabbing cash. Stolen hubcaps off unsuspecting cars got you five bucks a pair, two bucks a single. A pulled purse off an elderly woman's arm on the street was a crapshoot. Gene had a sniffer for knowing when there was a cashed Social Security check. There was no such thing as online banking. What a jungle.

Gene's brother finally threw me out. "Where's Gene?" I asked. "He was booked for knifing a woman in the tenement." Sure enough, Gene and his street buddy Tony Carlucci had been on a romp for drug cash. Their victim paid the ultimate price and years later Gene would as well, in Sing Sing prison in upstate New York. I never had any interest in, or use for, drugs. And that single factor probably saved my life. In any event, it was time for me to head back to Westchester, New York. I had ducked a big bullet and I knew it. I wafted between Wykagyl Country Club and Ellen and

Russ's house. Myrtle was a jewel and told me when the parents were gone, all the while loving Umpy. Truly, the most amazing woman.

At Wykagyl Country Club, I caddied and taught swimming. As a waiter, I had great meals from the kitchen and met a ton of interesting people. I often slept in the swimming-pool supply room and one morning was awakened by the golf pro. Claude Harmon was a god at the club and pros from all over came to him for lessons. His son, Butch, needed swimming lessons. (He would go on to be Tiger Woods's coach in later years.) When I caddied for Claude and his "student," I would get five dollars for a double golf bag. Jack Nicklaus gave me ten bucks. A good guy.

I was coming to the end of my senior year at the prep, working, and what could go wrong? Remember Ruddy and his bleeding cutting episode at the house? Well, that pretty much did it for me. I kept working but stopped going to classes. No big deal, right? Graduation was only a few days away.

Chapter Five

Beg To Die

When you find yourself in a hole, don't ask for a shovel!
- Me

In desperation, one finds.
- Yiddish proverb

Does everyone have that "special moment" in their lives? You know, the one that either makes or breaks you? Perhaps it's an illness, car accident, broken love, missed goal, or anything else that just plain hurts. How do you deal with it? Do you survive, for the better or the worse? It might be where Nietzsche's axiom came from: "If it doesn't kill you, it makes you stronger." I've come to learn the real meaning is that if it doesn't kill you, it only delays the inevitable. So do something to keep moving forward, even working shifts at Starbucks. It doesn't matter as long as it's moving you.

My moment came at the end of high school. My grades clearly sucked but I had enough credits to graduate. I was, as the song says, looking for love in all the wrong places. A typical male hormone-driven liar, I "loved" everyone, or so I said. But the year was ending and I was unscathed, without an offspring or a disease. It goes to prove that even fools get lucky now and then.

So summer is here. Tommy is one week from graduation. But I'm not in class. Where do I get the gown? When and where is the ceremony? Time for a call to the prep registrar's office. And here we go, the worst call any teenager can get. "Mr. Schneider, I have been trying to reach you. [No cell phones existed in 1963.] You are not qualified to graduate. School rules require that every student complete every course including the final exams, regardless of how many credits you may have." Nauseated, sick, sweaty, faint, I panicked. What the hell can I do? This is serious shit time. The war in Vietnam was raging. I felt totally alone. No words describe the searing feeling of despair. Years later I would land a high-performance fighter plane on an aircraft carrier, with a pitching deck, at night, in the rain. No lie, there isn't more adrenaline flow doing anything else. But that first-time landing on a carrier was high-test pure adrenaline: excitement, focus, and, yes, fear, all mixed in a delicious salad. The call letting me know I would not be graduating, though, left me despondent, horrified, and terrified. And did I mention pissed? Hell yes, I was angry. It would take a while for me to realize that we dig our own holes.

I couldn't see a way out. No home to go to for understanding and comfort. No friends, no money to speak of, and no plan for how to survive. But survive I must. Grandma was still stuck in my head. So I went for what we all need in a situation like that. I needed food, warmth, money, and a smile. Only one route to go: back to Wykagyl Country Club. There was a paycheck and place to rest and avoid the rain. I could caddy, teach swimming, and be a waiter at night. The hardest part was putting up with the incredibly wealthy clientele. Nothing was ever enough for them. The coffee was too hot! "Oh, so sorry, ma'am. I'll take it back." Mentally I was saying to myself, "Bitch. Can't you just sit there and continue rambling on inanely while your goddamned coffee cools off?" But nobody is stupid enough to lose their job over that. Not even I! Smile and sickeningly compliment them. Those two attributes would bring in the tips. And tips were my new panacea. The tips made the difference between kitchen leftovers and a real burger at Roy Rogers fast food.

After a week or two, my breathing was slowing to normal. Food, sleep, money, drunk middle-aged lonely housewives flirting with the teenage lifeguard with the bronze tan. It was heavenly to have shed some of the despair and anxiety. I knew well that I would have to do something to move forward, but had no clue what it would be. And then my Sunday karma came. I was sitting in the lifeguard chair, swinging my whistle around my finger. One had to look cool, after all. Suddenly I felt a tug on my leg, and looking down saw Ellen and Russ on the pool deck. They weren't members and were dressed as if coming from church. On a summer pool deck they looked like a pair of wine stains on a bride's white wedding gown. My dad sternly asked me to come down, and of course the pool patrons were all eyes. But this was not so embarrassing for me. I was shocked to see them both angry and tearful. They had just come from the Prep graduation and, not seeing me or hearing my name announced, went to the headmaster, Father Eugene O'Brien. He explained my sins and they were embarrassed and crushed. Russ's brother had accompanied them as well, to complete the legacy graduation. Tom had really screwed the day and their lives forever. There were the obligatory questions of "why" and "couldn't I have saved them the embarrassment?" I said nothing. I thought about

"I'm sorry," but I couldn't muster that lie. I watched them walk off the pool deck trying to miss the puddles. I guess that chlorine must kill the shine on shoes. It is pure wickedness on my part to admit the inner joy that I felt as I saw them leave and knowing I had made a great blow for freedom and revenge. Only years later would I learn that revenge is a double-edged sword. I don't know where it came from, but the saying "A man desiring revenge needs to dig two graves" is gospel truth.

So much credit goes to Diane at this time. I was dating her and had invited her to the prom. She agreed to go even though I wouldn't be graduating. Her parents, high-end socialites, were more than threatening to her. Maybe she thought it would assure her a better place in heaven. They were hard-core Catholics. Four years later we were married. I wore jeans and a jacket to the prom. Damned if I was going to rent a tux. At first, I felt like a leper at the dance. But in no time, most of my classmates came up to me and congratulated me. "Who the f--- needs a freaking diploma anyway?" Of course a number of the "key" students avoided me. They were the top students and, for them, it was best to stay away. Leprosy is potentially contagious. All in all, not a bad evening. I wanted to send my only other non-graduate buddy, Gene Cotes, a note, but I didn't want to interrupt his "yard time" at Sing Sing. Simply another reminder of how damned lucky I really was.

For the weeks that followed, I stayed at Wykagyl. Claude Harmon was good to me and every so often he'd slip me a "fin" (five bucks). Putting up with the privileged members was royally angering for me but the environment was safe. Compliment and smile: Tips were pouring in.

It would be a lie to say that there was no anxiety as the summer was coming to a close. I still had a ton of fun wherever I could find it. A fellow I met was playing guitar at the Beechmont Bar and Grill in New Rochelle. Nice laid-back chap who somewhat envied my position and only god knows why. That should have been a clue that he was nuts, but I was enjoying anyone who would listen to my plight. Anyway, Don the guitarist paid me five bucks to help set up at the bar. He was a great guitarist and I was damned near tone-deaf. What a pair. And one night his rhythm player couldn't show so Don taught me six chords on a cheap Stellar guitar and asked that I play backup. Backup? I didn't even know what "front up" was. But why the hell not. I played as softly as possible with a Marlboro hanging from my bottom lip. I must have played harder after a few beers because my strumming right fingers were bleeding after the show. The strings of his guitar were covered in blood. I felt like a bloody rock star.

Why does any of that matter? Oh, I forgot to mention that "Don" was Don McLean of "American Pie" fame. Yes, the one and only. He decided to join the Tommy club and quit school as well. Not sure if he ever went back and graduated from Iona Prep, his school. I lost touch with him as life became more chaotic for me.

None of that summer was enough to ease the queasy stomach I had as the summer job was coming to an end. What the hell could I do?

Remember that "life changer" moment I mentioned earlier? Mine was right around the corner. It would be the time of my life; a wanting-to-die time of my life and the greatest time of my life. I swear I remember it as if it happened yesterday. Word for word. It happened 60 years ago.

The summer was steamy hot and the best time of the day was 10:00 p.m. The pool was closed, the restaurant almost empty during the week although awash with booze and loaded club members on the weekends. It was my time to turn off the pool lights and go for a swim. It was heaven. I dove for the bottom at the deep end, holding my breath for as long as possible while sitting on the bottom. I could never figure out how you could kill yourself that way because when I needed air, nothing was going to stop me from racing to the surface for oxygen. There was no way to stay down there. Why was I even thinking that way? Did I mention that my life sucked? And it was about to get worse.

As the summer was ending, the teenagers were all talking about college and what it would be like to be away. I wasn't a genius, but was smart enough to know that this was no life for me. I needed to be in school, and I was quick enough to know that college was not an option without graduating from high school. I really needed help. And when one needed help in those days, you went to god. So off I went to talk to god or his representative. There was no plan. No premeditated words. No hint of how to approach His Holiness, but off I went to Fordham Prep to meet with Father Eugene O'Brien. He was the closest thing to god that I would ever know.

Blue jeans, a soiled white tee shirt with stains from the kitchen, with Keds high-top sneakers, and one scared s---less young boy sat in the vestibule of O'Brien's office. His secretary informed me that he couldn't see me for at least an hour. Hey, I was "going nowhere, doing nothing as a nobody," to quote Ellen. But I was barely indenting the chair's leather seat cushion when Father Eugene came out, looked directly at me and said, "Tom."

"Yes, Father," I said as I stood to approach him and shake his hand.

With not much else in my arsenal, manners were my forte. He said, "Please come in and have a seat." I swear that I have never felt so helpless and petrified. No words can describe how stripped naked I felt.

I entered the hallowed chamber of Father O'Brien and he pointed me to a lush leather sofa in front of his desk. The room smelled sanctimonious, like the sacristy behind the altar of a church. The room was filled with crucifixes and statues. I should have known whom they represented, but at the time I was the only one needing representation. And then came the fateful words from Father Eugene. "What the hell were you thinking? You completely missed the last three weeks of school as well as your graduation." I could feel it in the air. This wasn't going to go well. O'Brien had steel-cold eyes that bored through me. His voice was a razor and his words brilliantly and precisely chosen. I started to cry.

For the next few moments, I have no recall of what Father Eugene was saying. There were phrases like, "Bad times for you, I know," and "misdirected parents," "your handicapped brother," and finally, "What do you want from me?" I continued to sob and grab gulps of air as I told him how desperately I needed to be in college. College would be my salvation. And in an instant came apparent salvation. Eugene looked at me and reiterated the obvious that I needed to graduate in order to be accepted to college. I had more than enough credits but I had failed to complete any final exams and thus hadn't technically finished any of my courses.

"But Father, do I need those because I have so many credits even without them?"

"Yes, Thomas, those are the rules here at the Prep." It was time to push the envelope. Sympathy. I was desperate. "Father, I just want to die. I can't take any more of this. I don't want to end up like Gene Cotes, Father." Silence. Steel glaring at me. Eye to eye. Was I bullshitting him? He was searching to see. But I was safe from the glare because my words were as true as could be. I won't say that Father Eugene softened, but his face and tone showed kindness. No mistaking it. And then the words I was literally dying to hear: "The answer Tom, is clear. You need a diploma from Fordham Prep." I said nothing but continued to gasp and sob. Years later I remember my desperation. He needed no affirmation from me. He could see the relief.

Father Eugene J. O'Brien, S. J., looked down at a drawer in his desk and opened it. His fingers ruffled through folders and, opening one, he pulled out an unsigned diploma. Gold emblem and all. I remember him reaching into his black priest garb jacket as he pulled out a stylish Sheaffer ink pen. It reminded me of my invisible-ink pen from grammar school. God, this had better not be a joke with more invisible ink for his signature! No, it was the real deal. He unscrewed the top and carefully wrote my name on the top of the diploma. He even asked for my middle name. There must be a god!

I could see my name on the diploma, and now for Eugene's signature. But he was staring at the diploma for forever, and then looked at me. "Tom, before I sign this, I have one question for you." Geez, a quiz. Please don't ask me for the speed of light or Avogadro's number for electrons. No such luck. He continued, "Tom, whom do we graduate from Fordham Prep?" I needed to clear my head. Dig deep, Tom. "You graduate Catholic boys, Father." That answer might not get me a win on a quiz show but might get me a signature. "No, Tom, incorrect." Incorrect? That's a word reserved for tests. Christ, this was my final exams! Okay, one more try. "You graduate

Christian leaders, Father." How can you go wrong with that answer coming straight from my undershorts? "No, Tom. Would you like the answer?" From my lips came a crisp, "Yes, sir." Silence for what felt like another year, and then, "Thomas, we graduate MEN!" The words were loud and piercing. "Men" was unmistakable and well aimed in my direction. "So here is your moment, Tom. Will you be Tommy or Thomas? Shall I sign this diploma right now? All your problems solved." Yes, yes, of course! Sign the damned thing and let me out of here. I'll never do another evil thing. Cut me some slack! Well, you can imagine all the affirming phrases racing through my head. But none were uttered. O'Brien, the brilliant bastard, continued, "Or will you choose to be a man and take responsibility for your actions? Because, Thomas, that's what men do. They take responsibility for the consequences of their actions. But say the word and I'll sign this diploma. I am a MAN of my word."

I put my face in my hands and sank into deep sorrowful crying. Time passed, and then Father O'Brien said, "Shall I sign?" I couldn't speak. I only shook my head. I remember shaking his hand goodbye as I left the office, feeling a tad faint. His secretary offered me water but I politely refused and walked out to the smell of a hundred-year-old Jesuit prep school. I walked out a man. But a desperate man without a diploma. And to this day I have no valid high-school diploma. Not that I'm bragging, but how many doctors do you know without a high-school diploma? Now you know one.

Years later, I would admire my timid decision to take the hard road, but I would never forget the misery that I felt then. But that shaking head of mine in O'Brien's office would leave me in a truly desperate state. Sleep was usually my relief and my haven from the hellhole I was in. But there was not much sleep to be had now. I needed a solid game plan for survival.

Chapter Six

The Lie

Not all falseness is lying and not all lying is falseness.
You just have to fake it until you make it.
- Me, again

It was definitely a godawful time. It was the hot summer of 1963 and most of my time was at Wykagyl, working and learning what young men learn at country clubs with wealthy bored women everywhere. Eating at my gut minute to minute was the fact that I had no plan. I had no life. I had no advice. I did have a brother now in Rhode Island at the Kennedy home for disabled children and another brother at Columbia Psychiatric Institute. It's hard to describe the lonely despair that I kept breathing, but suffice it to say, dying was definitely a Plan D for me. The problem was that I didn't have Plans A, B, or C.

I'm not sure how the thought came to me, but suddenly a game plan started to form. All those years of religious training and downright "holy" crap never really leave you and I was still steeped in it. The war would change all that, but not for years to come. Because theology was such a huge part of my life and past, naturally the god thing would be a major part of the plan.

There were a few facts that I was able to formulate and verify. First, Jesuits were truly brilliant dudes and their program was extensive, tedious, and a brotherhood, much like a family. To become a diocesan (parish) priest, the requirement was four years of college and four more in the seminary learning priestly talents. But to become a Jesuit, after college was Jesuit seminary. This required ten to 12 more years, fluency in Latin and ancient Greek, a Ph.D. and a capacity to handle "spirits." Yes, the pun is intended.

Hey, wait a holy second. I like "spirits" and learning. Hell, maybe they'd allow a "trot" for the Latin and Greek classes. Chastity? Obedience? At this point in my life, I'd give it a shot. Worst scenario, it would give me a home for a few years and a college education. Yup, brilliant. Now we're cooking. Plan A.

And at that time, Holy Cross was the crème de la crème Jesuit academic center and a first segment to becoming a Jesuit priest. Best of all, it was free if you were a Jesuit novice (newbie priest-to-be). Seriously, was that genius planning or not? And the funny thing of it all was that it didn't really require my fabulously honed skills of lying. Somewhere deep inside, I felt I'd make a great priest. I desperately wanted a "family" that might actually be a fast track to heaven. The heaven-hell-god belief was still alive and well in me. Admittedly, it was rapidly fading. I was fascinated with theology and philosophy and read all I could grasp voraciously. The deeper I delved into those philosophical pages, the more insane my earlier beliefs became. But for that time, I could hedge a bit and believe that a life of philosophical theology and searching would be good for me.

Three square meals a day sounded very enticing. So I was not lying to myself as much as bending my inner truth. Okay, I was lying.

As I looked out over the pool, I was giddy knowing that I now had the hint of a plan. But did you ever commit to jump off the high-diving board when you were a kid? Gutsy decision, but how the hell was it going to turn out? While you stood at the end of the board, people were looking. You were seriously scared. You knew you had to jump, but maybe not right that second. Ah, procrastination can be such a comforting hug. I was on the end of my life diving board and I couldn't see any water in the pool, and felt only my shaking knees. If I didn't land upright with this "wanna be a Jesuit" stunt, I was already planning on going to Jones Beach in Long Island and swimming out to sea. I doubt that I would have taken that swim, but day-to-day life was getting desperate.

It was the end of August and I was off on Monday. I pulled together my cash and headed to the Port Authority in Manhattan. I must have looked like warmed-over Hamburger Helper in jeans and a Hawaiian short-sleeved shirt. Damned if I didn't look like the cat's meow. I remember that my bus was leaving for Worcester, Massachusetts, at midnight on Sunday. I had a pocket full of change for the array of soda and goodies in the vending machine in the bus center. I remember that "Good and Plenty" candy was my serotonin of choice. A box of pink and white candies, a Coke, and my flip-top red box of Marlboros and I was ready to jump, but the knees were still shaking. I boarded the bus and sat on the smokers' side. I never understood how half the bus was for smokers and the other half for health nuts. A real genius must have come up with that smoking arrangement.

I don't remember much of the ride because there was nothing to see. It was pitch-dark and there were no more than six or eight other passengers. I was the lone rider to Worcester. That should have been a hint to me about the vibrancy of Worcester. But I was on my way to drink in Plan A. Maybe.

The bus station in Worcester was a half-hour walk from the campus of Holy Cross, and the kindness of people at the station directed my trek. My first thoughts on the walk would be confirmed in the years to follow. The sun had come up and the crisp air told me that fall was creeping in. My first thought was damn, this is one hilly place! It was around 6:30 in the morning on Tuesday and I entered the gate to Holy Cross College. It was absolutely beautiful, like nothing I had ever seen. Lush green full trees, well-trimmed grass, more brick buildings than I could count, and, oh yes, hills.

I was stopped at the entrance gate by a security guard, later to be known as a campus cop. "Are you a student? Student I.D.?" "No, sir." "Well, son, it's 6:45 in the morning. What are ya here for?" I replied with a confident, "I'm here to become a Jesuit priest, sir, and I need to find the rectory."

I think the 'priest' thing got him because he pointed me up the hill (naturally) and to the last building on the left. I could see it from the front gate and it was nothing less than formidable. So up I trekked. Man, what a hike and no chance to hitch a ride from a passing driver. I'm not sure that even god was awake at that hour. I would soon learn that a Jesuit day started two hours earlier.

The rectory was a cut stone and brick building, Gothic but not ostentatious at all. I'd be lying if I told you I felt cool, calm, and collected. I felt more like Barney Fife, the deputy on *The Andy Griffith Show*. I don't know how long it took me to lift and lower the door knocker, but after a tad I raised it, and the knocker felt like 20 pounds of black iron. It didn't take a minute for the door to creak open, and standing in the doorway was a huge man in priestly garb.

"Yes, son, how may I help you?"

Oh my god, showtime! This was happening and it was for real. Don't blow this, Tommy, because this is your one and only chance.

"Good morning, Father. I'm Tom Schneider and I'm here to become a Jesuit priest."

Dead silence. Dead silence for a year or so, it seemed. "Please come in, Tom. Do you know how to serve at Mass?" "Yes, Father." "Excellent. Let's go to the chapel and you can serve my Mass." I remember walking to the chapel and running through my old Church Latin liturgy in my head. I mused, what the hell is a kid who was stealing hubcaps two weeks ago doing serving Mass?

Mass went well with only a few blurps from me to cover up forgotten liturgy. Back at the rectory, Father Joe Donahue, as he had introduced himself earlier, led me to the kitchen. We sat in a luscious kitchen with huge hanging pots and pans, large iceboxes (refrigerators), and a massive gas stove and oven. Questions came quickly and my answers were not slowed by my chewing on bacon.

It's hard to recall what was said by either of us that morning, but I tried desperately to explain my prior life and current goals. Father Joe was such a kind man and so attentive I couldn't help but fill a chunk of my story with pure heartfelt crying. I'm sure that my outpouring was purely due to the amazing empathy that this man of god was showing toward me. There wasn't a single fiber of my body that wasn't screaming at my mind, "Stop this crap! You have no desire to live a celibate chaste life." And so the story continued into the late afternoon. For those interested, lunch was delicious. Clam chowder, grilled cheese, and ice cream. Yes, I still remember. Such a difference from the Twinkies and Yoo-hoo drinks that normally sustained me. It felt like being in the Wykagyl kitchen stealing food off of the used dinner plates of the elite. Learning Principle number one: Jesuits eat well and drink well. Not a bad learning tool.

I'll never know why Father Joe took that chance on me, but his innate kindness had to be the major reason. I do know that at the end of the day, he came to me after a 30-minute "by myself" time, and he said that he had spoken to Father O'Brien and that he had confirmed my family story. Not sure if O'Brien mentioned my foray with Father Pat from years before, but the final score was Jesuits, zero, and Tommy, one. Yes, I won. I would be accepted without a high-school diploma and had six days to get my physical exam and its form signed and return to campus before classes began. I would be living in O'Kane rectory on the top floor. Did I mention there was no elevator? Naturally! Nonetheless, I was in!

Now doesn't that sound easy? Well, it sure as hell wasn't. Where would I go for six days? I didn't have enough cash to go back to the city and return to Worcester. So it was off to the library for me. It didn't take long to find areas to sleep in among the stacks of books. The students weren't back yet, so the dorms were empty and the showers available. Food? Down to the dining hall and a few well-placed lies about being a regular student back early from summer recess. No problem, because lunch and dinner were being served that week on a limited basis. Breakfast? For breakfast, I sneaked into the chapel and searched the sacristy (behind the altar) and stole a handful of hosts and a few swigs of wine and water. The hosts were unleavened bread and swelled in my stomach, the result resembling a full course meal. I was never sure if the hosts had been consecrated (blessed into the body and blood of Christ) which would have been the height of sacrilege, a mortal sin condemning me to the fires of hell forever. At least I wouldn't be on the hell train hungry. I was happy as a clam and, at that time, would have been happy to live that way forever, or at least until I could find a better gig. The only thing missing in my life was a long hit on a Marlboro. Sometimes I found a snuffed butt in an ashtray and I'd relight it. Lots of the Jesuits (also called "Jevies") smoked, so all in all, pretty safe. I certainly didn't catch any extra religiosity.

How to get my physical exam form signed? Compared to my past hike to get where I was, a forged signature was a no-brainer. I did have to copy the handwriting from the signers of the Declaration of Independence. I chose Hamilton's handwriting because it was so large and easy to see. I can't remember the doctor's name, but I recall spending time on it. Not Hamilton. Too close to the signature. Not Smith; too stupid. I think it was something like Walzik. No reason except that it sounded and looked good. And that was that. Books to read, plenty of food to eat, and an occasional lucky find of a cigarette butt.

Eventually the students started trickling back in. I met them during meals and knew immediately that I sure didn't belong there. Most of the guys were Catholic and from Catholic prep schools. They looked wealthy and cute. Cute meaning J. Crew, Abercrombie & Fitch model cute. Cocky and arrogant were the tattoos they could have been sporting. But they didn't have tattoos. Why? Because tattoos hurt, and "hurt" sure as hell wasn't in their vocabulary. Many went on to become well-known politicians, lawyers, and doctors. I never seemed to fit in, even now. That wasn't a problem for the first year and a half because my time was spent with the Jevies and a stack of philosophy books cornered by ancient Greek and Latin texts. Yes, I can be the real hit of a party with those skills. Or maybe not.

So there I am with three squares every day, a black cassock gown to wear that would have gotten me shivved (knifed) in the Bronx, and brilliant men with whom to discuss the questions of life every night. I can still smell the tobacco-scented leather chairs in the "evening room" of the Jevies. It was Socrates' playroom with Saint Ignatius Loyola (the founder of the Jesuits) as the emcee. I had never known so much warmth, security, and peace in my life. A Disney cruise? No, comfort wasn't part of the package. In fact, it was anathema for me to show joy or comfort to my superiors. Similar to the military, as a newbie I was expected to work, study, and appear somewhat dour. That was my role. It would be years before I could enjoy the benefits of being a Jesuit professor at Holy Cross. As time went on, I saw that most of those benefits as an ordained Jesuit came down to a few perks: a peaceful life, wine and brandy, no stress, the joy of teaching, and the camaraderie of fellow priests entrenched in the belief and work of god. Unfortunately, I still had a fire in my belly. Anger and the need for an adrenaline rush were pulsing through my blood vessels. And somehow the religious fervor of the past was rapidly fading. The Jesuits had been very, very good to me, but all of my prior experiences with religion and the religious were incredibly contradictory compared to the actual theology of the Church. I wanted all of the myths and religiosity to be true. But every religious glitch took a piece of my soul. For instance, as a child, I had my father demanding daily Mass, weekend rosaries, and proclaiming the infallibility of priests and the Church. On the other side, I remember joining the Boy Scout troop at my grammar school, Immaculate Conception. At ten years old, wearing that uniform and using knives and tents was a young boy's dream. I took it seriously and climbed the ranks quickly. There was a large campout over one weekend and I was excited. We all drove to the woods several miles from school. A sleepover in tents, for god's sake; now we're talking. Naturally it started to rain, and the tents were old canvas with a fantastic moldy well-used smell. I loved it. It would make me gag today, but it was like Old Spice aftershave lotion back then. I was in a tent with three other boys and by the time we were set up, I was pretty hungry. I donned my poncho and headed out to see the rest of the camp. Walking with my trusty flashlight I felt like Daniel Boone, albeit hungry. Through the bushes, there was another camp of Scouts. I headed there and was met by some Scouts from a Baptist church. They offered me a hot dog, which I gladly accepted. I wolfed it down and took another one to bring back to my tent. I felt great. I went into the tent and was immediately accosted by the other tent mates.

"What's that smell?!"

Have you ever been really hungry and someone throws a burger on a grill? Man, you can smell it for a mile. And within minutes, Father O'Malley popped into our tent with our dinner, carrying a stack of American cheese in one hand and a loaf of bread in the other.

"What's that smell in here, boys?"

"Tommy has a hot dog, Father."

"True, Tommy?"

"Yes, Father, but I had only one. I was going to share the other."

"Tom" (going from being called Tommy to Tom wasn't a good sign), "today is Friday and it's a mortal sin to eat meat on Friday!"

What does a hot dog cost? I'll tell you. It cost me being kicked out of the Scouts and Father O'Malley driving me home the next morning. A delightful drive in silence, broken only by Father's reminder that if I died before confessing my sin, I would go straight to hell. A ludicrous spit at my age now, but I can assure you that at ten, it was a week of massive diarrhea. Of course, my father took it well. No, I was going to take it well! Take what? The belt. At least that smacking was a belting in the privacy of his bedroom. Hurt? Not close to the hurt of being kicked out of the Scouts. I still have my Scout manual, "Tenderfoot." But what goes around comes around. I was scheduled to go to confession later in the week. At the close of your session in the confessional booth, the priest asks if you are truly sorry for your sins. Sorry? I was damned sorry—to have been caught. And how stupid to say to 'god' that I was sorry for eating a hot dog on Friday night? The universe must have roared with laughter. The come-around was that 40 years later my son Mark joined the Scouts and became an Eagle Scout. I'm not embarrassed to say that I teared up at his Eagle ceremony. Amazing. I should have celebrated with a Nathan's hot dog.

But I digress. Back on the hill of Holy Cross I continued to play the role. Admittedly, I was becoming more and more of a nonbeliever, but I truly respected and loved my new family of Jesuits. I really hated to fake it in front of these amazingly devoted men, but I knew the time was coming. My biggest hint was finding myself daydreaming during morning and night prayers. The daydreams were consistently about the gorgeous coeds that I saw from the bus as I went to town for necessities. Soon my necessities turned more into getting off the bus in front of the girls' Catholic college, Anna Maria College. It didn't take long to realize that a black cassock was definitely not a chick magnet. Okay, with a little confidence, I snuck out to the bus in jeans. It didn't take long to meet a few coeds and to be invited onto their campus for coffee. On one such visit, I met a stunning young woman named Della. And I do mean stunning. She was runner-up for Miss Rhode Island in the Miss America contest. Why me? Was it devastating charm and good looks? Not a chance. I was the original carbon copy of Jerry Lewis crossed with Clem Kadiddlehopper. (Not to feel bad if you don't recall Clem. He was a character performed by the comedian Red Skelton. You don't remember Red Skelton? Ask your parents.) I was feeling pretty good about my charm until her girlfriend told me that she had just broken up with her lifelong boyfriend. Rebound phenomenon. I sure didn't care. She was dazzling. She was gorgeous and not the brightest crayon in the box. I didn't care. There were all the brains I could ever cope with back at the Cross. I would have cared, though, had I known that her ex was the son of the Mafia boss in Rhode Island and owner of the Lincoln Downs racetrack. I couldn't invite her to the Holy Cross campus for anything! I was studying to be a priest, and it turns out they don't date coeds!

My bus rides became more frequent and Della and I spent more time in the school's basement bowling alleys that no one ever used. We spent hours doing what young thoughtless teens do, but Della was getting serious. She slipped in words about marriage, babies, and cottages. Whoa! Suddenly my brain started to focus, and panic was setting in. How could this end gently? Nothing else in my life ever had ended nicely and neither would this.

One night after 10:00 prayers, my answer arrived. I was lying in my bed feeling pretty good about life and only slightly concerned about Della. Like a lollipop, you want to put it down, but it tastes so damned good.

KNOCK, KNOCK on my chamber door. Loud knocking, disconcerting. I sleepily opened the door to see Father Doyle and two Rhode Island state troopers. Christ! My pulse was in Atlas rocket mode and my mind was soaring. What in the hell had I done?

After the usual questioning of "who," "age," and "Did I know Della?" the story came out. Her ex was the son of Mr. Dario. It turns out that "Mr. D.," as he was referred to by the troopers, was head of the Mafia and his son had heard that I was dating his son's girlfriend. His son had sworn to come to the Cross and blow me away. Bang bang. Had I been contacted by him? No. Did I know what he looked like? No. Father Doyle never interrupted, never said a word. Where was my John Wayne routine now that I needed it? Nowhere. The troopers said that they had been posted by Mr. D. to stem any conflict. Conflict? Me dead? A tad more than conflict. They would post plainclothes guards at my door and the doors of the rectory. Great! Sleep was only a moment away. Not a chance. The watch went on for about a day and Mr. D.'s son was caught, not with a gun but with a switchblade in his pocket. A tool I was quite familiar with.

When the police were gone only the many questions of "What did you do?" remained. This did make it easy for me to call Della saying how much I thought of her but that I was crazy in love with my life. Tears and god knows what at the other end of the phone, but it was over. Well, not quite.

It was probably a week before the fateful envelope was at my door, just enough time to pass for the "all clear" whistle to sound. But the envelope was from Father Joe and contained a request to meet with him in his office after classes. Okay, nothing too bad so far. As I walked into his office, I was relatively calm. Father Joe's demeanor made that easy. I sat in his plush leather chair as Father Joe tamped his pipe and lit up. Oh, how I loved the smell of his pipe. Better than incense. Father Joe kept the mood with his dulcet calming voice. As I watched the wafting smoke from his pipe, he went through the usual how's it going and how was my path, and the kicker, "Do you have anything to say to me, Tom?"

"No, Father, everything's fine." Father Joe then proceeded to tell me in firm but not angry words that this path is a vo-cation and not a va-cation. Ah, the Jesuit uppercut. I was dead and there was no way to con Father Joe. I respected him and owed him too much. Damn! Another family gone, and how would I live without my Jevies, particularly Father Joe, clearly the kindest man I had ever met. Humble and brilliant. What to do?

I started to cry. Real gut-ache crying. I explained how my intentions were truly sincere and that I tried my best. He agreed and simply stated that this life is not for everyone and perhaps it would be mine again, later in life. I knew that wouldn't happen with all the Dellas of the world needing my personal help in ancient Greek, Latin, and philosophy! But what do I do? The Vietnam war was raging but the American furor of it had not peaked. I would be launching for sure.

"You'll stay here at the Cross, Tom, and finish college. You'll have to pay back the school for your tuition, of course. We'll find you a room with one of the students." Good god, there must be a god! But I should have known that if I was going to room with someone at this point in the year and a half since classes began, the guy didn't have any roommate for a reason. And sure enough, there

I was checking into the dorm with "Phil." Phil in a nutshell was a narcissistic, misogynistic, arrogant liar. (No, he didn't become the president.) His day started when he looked in the mirror and kissed his flexed biceps. Seriously. We were at war from day one. Simple crap like him saying, "I don't like the smell of your deodorant." "Phil, that's not my deodorant. I have amazingly ambrosially aromatic flatulence!" That Greek and Latin did come in handy. I had to get out. Out of the Cross, but first, out of Phil's view. I bet he runs a string of Gold's Gyms today. And then, as with all of my life, fate stepped in to re-align the map.

I had been out on the campus trying to get a hold of my life on a freezing cold night. Snow was on my breath and I was craving a Marlboro. I hated being at Holy Cross and yet I had no alternative. "Suck it up, Tommy boy," I told myself. Walking back into the dorm with most students sleeping, I headed to the room I shared with psycho Phil. But a few doors before mine I saw a student sitting on the floor of the corridor with his forehead on his knees and sobbing. I remember stopping and thinking, "Just keep walking, Tommy. You don't need this." I honestly don't know, to this day, why I sat on the floor next to him, but I did. He was John. John didn't say anything; he only sat there crying. I sure knew that feeling. It didn't matter why he was crying. I knew the hurt. After some time I took him by the arm and said, "If you're gonna cry, you oughta do it with a friend. Let's go." Up we went into his room. He spent most of the night crying and I'd love to tell you why, but he's been my best friend for 55 years and I've never asked. I sat at his desk while he lay in his bed and we both cried. He never asked why I was crying. It didn't matter. We were now friends for life.

Chapter Seven

John

"the meek shall inherit the earth"
- Jesus

"A friend in need . . . " First, what the heck is the meaning of a true friend? If I have a couple of six-packs of Coors and chips with cheese dip, I've got friends knocking on my door. Add a football game on a wide-screen TV and I suddenly have too many "friends." No, what I'm talking about is being able to pick up the phone and asking your true friend for a kidney. A true friend instantly says, "What day and what time?" A true friend doesn't ask you why or say "I'm so sorry." He or she doesn't use words. They use their shoes to meet you at the hospital. True friends are harder to find than Bin Laden. Now, I haven't had to make that call nor have I received one. But here's the thing. I have the phone number of a true friend who would pick up the phone immediately: John.

John and I should never have become friends. And to this day, I have no idea why I sat down and cried with him. I had enough problems of my own without taking on somebody else's. Maybe all I needed was a good cry. In any event, crybabies united.

John and I came from different planets. His parents were the kindest, most caring parents I had ever met. His dad was the mayor of Rockville Centre on Long Island and his forte was that he loved to laugh. John's mom was straight off the set of *Father Knows Best.* For those too young to remember, that show represented the example of family living as we all wish it existed. John's mother made you believe such a family could exist. She smelled like chocolate-chip cookies and was Betty Crocker in making them.

John had attended Catholic grammar school and he bought into most of the Church's teachings. Although liberal in his religiosity and politics, he had lived a sheltered life. And then there was Tommy suddenly in his life. His world was about to expand. My life was about to be tempered and my anger, abated.

John had an amazing asset for Holy Cross College. He had a car! Wheels! I still hadn't even gotten my license. But I could sure drive and there was no need for John to know about some of my other escapades that left me without a license. I felt like Ferris Bueller looking at his friend's father's Ferrari. John's car was nicknamed "Progeria." Progeria is an incredibly unfortunate disease that affects newborns. The infant ages at warp speed and ultimately dies as a child. We put so many miles on that car, eventually the only thing that worked on it was the ashtray.

I loved John for so many things, but his humble demeanor, brilliant mind (hidden by a cloud of goofiness), and love of laughter topped the list. To see him move on this planet was like watching a mechanical Tinkertoy self-destruct. His feet pointed to various points on the compass with every step. Would he make it down the hall? Vegas would call it an even bet, at best. But put a golf club in his hand and you were now looking at Arnold Palmer. I swear. The man swung a club like few ever could. I had caddied for some of the best at Wykagyl Country Club including Arnie Palmer, Jack Nicklaus, and Lee Trevino. John wanted to see their autographs and I told him that I never asked. I only wanted my "fin" for carrying the bag. John was a flowing waltz when he played golf. Unfortunately, I hated golf from my previous country-club experiences. I so wanted to bond with John that I told him I'd give it another try. For hours, we went out in the dorm corridor to putt golf balls into cups. I actually got to be pretty decent. On to the big clubs. John didn't think I was ready for a "driver," but I could certainly handle a yardstick. And so after a putting session, I swung the yardstick. Hey, I'm not kidding. I cranked the yardstick with eyes down and hips moving with knees. Perfect. After weeks, I was ready. John treated me to a bucket of balls at the driving range. I was on a cloud. Maybe I could even make the golf team. Easy, big boy; let's get through the bucket first.

At the driving range, I placed my first ball on a little white nipple in the center of a fake green mat. John stood opposite to watch me and had me check my stance and take a few practice swings. No problem. Move over, Arnie. Whoops! My first real swing and the ball missed John's eye by a few inches! How the hell could that have happened? John politely agreed. It was an impossible shot, but he thought it best that he stand behind me. I told you he was smart.

My golf never got any better, but I was proud to caddy for John in his tournaments in school. Walk miles to hit a little white ball into a hole? Too crazy for me. Sorry.

But John wasn't only a good friend with whom I could share a meal. No, he was truly my source of sanity. I absolutely loved to screw with him. All in fun, but suddenly I had a playmate. I remember typical cons with John. At one point in November of 1966, we were debating as to which of us was the more manly. A typical question for two dorks who didn't belong at Holy Cross. The answer would require a manly test. I told John that we should hit the community shower in our dorm and get into opposite shower stalls. Once soaked, we would lower the water temperature to as cold as we could handle. As soon as one of us quit and jumped out, we would switch showers and get in each other's to see which was colder. Seemed that I had come up with a purely scientific, and may I add genius, experiment to prove manliness. John was all in. It was already freezing at the Cross with a snow-covered campus. John finally ran out of the shower and I was grimacing and moaning in freezing pain. The problem was that I was faking and had never turned my shower down. John jumped in my shower and I walked out and toweled off. John started laughing and enjoyed the rest of a warm shower. I think he might have used the word "bastard" but my memory fails me. Naïveté. Had John any experience, he would have known about "shrinkage." I had none and John had so much that he could have passed for female. I am happy to report that there was no permanent damage to John.

I had taken a weekend job at a pizza shop, but money was very tight. John actually had a credit card and cash. Unbelievable from my view. But whenever we'd walk by the soda machine, I'd put in my quarter and slam the Sprite button and John would whack the Coke. I always won, and John would get lightly frustrated. One day, I had no quarter. John suggested he'd put in his quarter and we'd slam together to see who'd win. "Alright," I said, "but since I always win I'll cut you some slack. I'll push the Coke and you hit the Sprite on the count of three." Okay: one, two, three! Slam! Yes, you know what happened. John slammed Sprite and I hit the machine but never touched the Coke button. I don't think John stopped laughing for half an hour. How can you not love a guy who has been duped, realizes it, and can heartily laugh at himself? That is John.

By the middle of our junior year in 1966, John knew me well and knew my family up and down. There were many school holidays that allowed me to ride to Long Island with John and enjoy his parents. And John would let me use his car to drive to Rhode Island to visit my brother Mark, and Myrtle his Jamaican nurse.

John loved the stories of my house and the stories within. I think it seemed like a Stephen King novel to him. How could there be such a family? He knew that Russ was the president of McCann-Erickson, a worldwide advertising company. They were the epitome of the recent TV serial about advertising in the 1950s, called *Mad Men*. As the leader in the field, McCann put on most of the early TV shows. As the oldest son of the president, I was asked to be on a number of the shows. Exciting? Not really. It meant a short haircut and makeup. Yuck. I did get to take Hayley Mills to her cotillion. Truth be told, I rode with her in a limo to the Waldorf Astoria. Once inside the hotel, there were flashbulbs everywhere and I was asked to move aside. That's the last of Hayley Mills and Tommy. I wonder if she still thinks of me?

Hayley Mills and others in that world whom I met reminded me of how serendipitous life really is. In high school, I would sneak out and suds up at a bar in New Rochelle. I was 16. Nobody cared at the Beechmont Bar and Grill. At night, different bands came in and touted their wares. Hence my hookup with Don McLean. I loved the Beechmont mainly for its smell and the atmosphere of the customers. I always asked Nick the bartender if I could take the drinks to a table. I felt like the real deal, a lot older than the punk kid that I actually was. The whole place smelled of spilled Budweiser and cigarette smoke. Unmistakable. I wonder if Hayley Mills would have been impressed? There I was carrying a tray of beers to a table. I wore a white tee shirt with my box of Marlboros wrapped up in my shirt sleeve. One James Dean look all wrapped up in a skinny package sans the muscles. Or so I thought.

John loved those stories and was hell-bent on having some of his own. Just in time, because along comes trouble with the name Tom.

One boring night in the late winter we decided to take a night ride in Progeria. We weren't allowed off campus after 10:00 p.m., so this jaunt excited John. Off we rode into the night in Progeria with one stop at a diner for burgers. As we left, there were six sticks of American cheese on a plate at the counter, and as John paid the bill, the cheese sticks went into my pocket. Not exactly a mortal sin, but no sense guilting John, so I kept them to myself until later.

We drove up a mountain road and Progeria started huffing and puffing. At the top of the path, the headlights went out. Pitch dark. I was driving and decided to "guts" it by going forward. We immediately shot down the other side of the hill but I couldn't see a damned thing. John was speechless. It was the downside of a rollercoaster, blind! When it all quieted down, both of us opened the doors and felt the snow on our faces. It didn't take long to realize that we were at a dead stop with 20-foot gullies on either side. Christ! Why weren't we dead? Okay, back in the car. Intermittently turning the heater on to keep from freezing, we both realized we had no clue where we were or what to do. Stay alive was goal number one.

Both of us were freezing and without sleep, and we were both hungry. I pulled out the almost frozen cheese sticks and shared them with John. They were amazing! Delicious and comforting. Sometimes theft pays off. John never questioned where or how they showed up. He just moaned, "magic cheese." And to this day, we drool over the words "magic cheese." The following morning, the sun came up like the Phoenix bird. We made it out and John had the electrical failure repaired. Moral of the story: Never enter the wilderness without magic cheese.

Most of our shenanigans were milder but just as dumb. For example, John had never been in a caboose. Who cares? I did. So in mid-spring of junior year, I took John down to the railyard in Worcester. We climbed the fence and in the dark made our way between train cars and finally came to a red caboose. We climbed up and into the deserted caboose, so cool that I remember it today. There was a potbellied stove, the thick smell of stale pipe smoke, and a long leather-cushioned feather bed. The leather was cracked, well-worn. It would get more use. John was ecstatic. I lit up one of my three Marlboros. Two guys in a caboose. Yes, there could be a god, and John was already firmly convinced of that. I was still on the fence about the god thing, but we'd have many heavy-duty chats about that in the future and, come to think about it, we do even today. Time to chat and nap. One of the talks would have been about Diane in Larchmont, New York. I was semi-dating her. In those days, if you were 21 and single, something wasn't right: Why aren't you married yet? Her family seemed fine and very very Catholic. John was supportive and he wasn't dating at all. Enough for me. Time to rest. We both fit on the ancient leather couch bed. In nothing flat, two guys were out cold.

John woke up first and in a panic. We were moving! Jesus! Where the hell were we going? Should we jump? I looked outside and we were really moving. A jump might cause a big-time injury. For once, good thinking. So we sat looking out, in mild panic. But truthfully, it was gorgeous. Stars through the skylights and towns whipping by. A vagabond's nomad dream. Right up my alley. John loved it too, but he was clearly worried about how we would get out of this mess. Not being back for classes would seriously affect my chance to stay in school. John was amazing and convinced his parents about the innocence of our adventure. As always, John's parents covered the flight back from—Chicago! Ah, the beauty of a credit card. An apologetic and thankful phone call from me was taken kindly by Mayor Anderson. Truth told, I think John's dad laughed inside and he might have been a tad jealous. Those were some amazing parents. I could never repay them.

It didn't take long to realize that money was a key to survival. You would think that with my background and present status, I would crave shekels. It should have been my prime focus. But Russ made a ton of money and all of his friends and associates were loaded as well. Ellen ran through money like faucet water through your fingers. In fact Ellen and Russ did have expenses: five kids in parochial schools, my brother Mark, and nursing care. But they still lived a damned great life washed heavily in brandy and gin and tonics. The kicker was that they weren't happy. Neither laughed, danced, or enjoyed life. Even when life was smooth, for them it was always a struggle. Perfect for a Catholic mindset. Throw in a hair shirt and a few rosaries, and you've got a chunk of heaven. I wanted none of that. Not the religion and not the money. It seemed to me that money helped to cause their misery and, by the domino effect, my misery. But religion was my lifeline and I hadn't figured out how to divest myself of it. All of that was whirling around and I knew I needed more money than the pizza shop gave me. I must admit, however, that the free pizza was better than any health plan.

What to do? And then another brainstorm hit me. It would soon become a lifelong brain fart. Walking home from a weekend walk with some slices of pepperoni pizza for John, I passed one of those "cheesy" (sorry, I'm recalling the pizza) ads for the U.S. Navy. "Enlist Now!" Why not? What have I got to lose? After all, I knew the West Point hymn by heart. Oh yeah, that was the Army.

Naturally I ran my idea past John, and he was dead set against it. I can't remember his reasons, but I'm sure they were spot-on. The final answer, however, was that I desperately needed the moolah. And that decision changed my life. I guess all of the paths we choose will change our lives. Of course, there was a war raging. None of us knew anything about the politics at that point. The meme throughout the country was that the communists were invading South Vietnam and their next attack would be on San Francisco. So it was a "just" war. So we needed to fight. It was our duty. We would all learn how insane that thinking was. That education for me was more than merely expensive.

Chapter Eight

Away for Anchors Aweigh

"Once a dork, always a dork!"

Sure, there was excitement walking into the Navy Recruiting Office that spring day, but I'd be lying if I denied having any trepidation. It didn't take long to undergo their physical and reams of paperwork. After all, I was fresh meat and the recruiters were given a week off for each individual recruited. I would be paid $132 every two weeks, working as an enlisted man at South Weymouth Air Station in Rhode Island for one weekend a month. That next summer I would enjoy a delightful summer in boot camp. What a deal! I had fallen into the best gig yet.

I had a hint about my future life back on campus. I was actually proud that I was in the military and so freely told some of my classmates. Some of them were in ROTC to become officers and they were quick to tell me what a jerk I was to be an enlisted man. As I have mentioned before, I surely didn't fit in at the Cross. The word spread, and I suddenly became a verbal piñata for their taunts. "Hey, squid shit, get out of my way." "Hey 'dixie cup' hat, kiss my ass." ("Dixie cup" was slang for the white hat sailors wore.) A true environment of gentlemen. Not all were derisive, but certainly the arrogant and privileged attitude of the students stung like a wasp bite.

Later, John and I would enjoy our own satisfaction. We had graduated from Holy Cross 25 years earlier. Neither one of us had maintained any connection to the school or our classmates. Okay, let's do it. Our 25th anniversary reunion. We agreed, although John was certainly skeptical about returning to the scene of the crimes and beehive of the elites. No problem, because I would handle the details. So I ordered our tickets for the various functions and even bought John a ticket for the golf tournament. Rooms for the weekend were in the student dorms with the students absent for summer break. It was 2002 and John was now a lead attorney for Toshiba and I was retiring from the Navy but now as a physician. The call for rooms was met with a courteous response that I was too late for a reservation. I felt as if I was being sent to detention for punishment. What would my penance be? Two "Hail Marys" and one "Our Father"? It was time to pull a Ferris Bueller move. So I told the administrator I was a physician. (For some stupid reason, that always makes laypeople snap to attention. Maybe they think I could medically hex them.) To seal the deal, I told them I would be bringing the oldest Holy Cross graduate to the reunion. John would suddenly be 91 years old and I was hoping to stay with this ancient graduate at the infirmary on campus. "Certainly, Doctor, and would there be anything else you'll be needing?" Amazing! Absurd b.s. wins over a white lie every time.

On the appointed summer day, I pulled up in front of John's house in a rented hearse. A red cross made of tape made it an official ambulance. As a doc, I brought an I.V. with tubing I taped to John's arm. Grey hair spray and a cane, and John was dawdling along as an old geezer. Off we drove to Massachusetts, much to the chagrin of John's wife, Kathleen. As I pulled out of John's driveway, I looked back and thought I saw Kathleen hotly glaring at me. No, it must have been only the way the noon sun was coating her face?

We arrived at about 10:00 p.m., which helped because it was dark. A nurse met us with all of the deference of "Welcome, Doctor, and please let me know if there's anything I can do to help." We were in! John got the bed and I had the miserable reclining chair next to it. What the hell, it was free. The next day was a blow off. Needless to say, we missed the morning Mass. John's hair was still dyed grey and it got him many a pathetic look, but John loved it.

I suggested that we visit a dorm and take a shower. We could see who was the real man. We could lower the shower temp to as cold as we could hack it. No! John reminded me that he looked old and was old but not senile. It went something like "Fool me once, shame on you"—you know the rest. And so we readied for the gala in the field house that night. It was a formal function and we were sans tuxes. No problem: jeans and a jacket would have to cut it. I had a brown bag filled with a few goodies. These included invisible ink. Yes, the same stuff I got in trouble for in grammar school. Early youth training pays off. I also had a few cans of squirting plastic string. Another favorite of mine. Loaded for bear, we were off to see our old best buddies from 25 years past.

It was a jaunt from the infirmary to the field house and we definitely were winded at the top of the hill. And there, waiting for us at the entrance, was a receiving line of our class elite. Chris Matthews (of *Hardball*), James Moran (congressman), and others were adorned in crisp tuxedos. There was a brisk order for us to turn and put on our name tags. God, I hate name tags, so that wasn't going to happen, but the turnaround was perfect to load up. I had the invisible ink and John had the spray string. Turning on cue, John fired, and I tossed and splashed the ink all over those lovely tux shirts. Do I need to explain the chaos and cursing that followed? You can make up your own, but it went something like, "You a--holes, get the f--- out of here." John and I turned to leave saying to each other things like "Something we said?" and "Do you think the string was too much?" We laughed all the way back to the infirmary and yee-hah, it was all downhill!

We went to the "Miss Woo" greasy-spoon diner in Worcester for breakfast and headed home. Kathleen was thrilled that John was home early, so maybe I scored a few points with her for that. John and I have never returned to the Cross, although we each donate to the school each year. A great school, just not for us. We were like two hamburgers at a vegetarian banquet.

At that time I was long since gone from the Navy and Pensacola Naval Hospital and Bethesda Naval Hospital and the National Institute of Health (Dr. Tony Fauci of COVID-19 fame's work center) were only a momentary memory. Now I was fully steeped in civilian practice and had survived an onslaught of medical catastrophes. Thanks so much, Vietnam and Agent Orange! John was back doing that lawyer thing. Returning to the world as a civilian reminded me of those first days as an enlisted man back in 1966. My weekend assignment at South Weymouth was cake. Granted, the pay wasn't great but I was driven there and was fed and bedded for the weekend. Yes, I can handle this. Whoops, I spoke too fast. I hadn't counted on a summer vacation, but summer was upon me and I was off to boot camp in Pensacola, Florida. I was flown to

Pensacola and it was my first time in a plane. I was ecstatic. A crappy box lunch on board and six and a half hours of a droning flight. No, there were no reclining seats or in-flight movies. I sat on web seats with about 20 other guys. Little did I know that the flight would be the best part of an upcoming eight weeks in hell. Boot camp was held in 98-degree temperatures and 90 percent-plus plus humidity. The introduction was meant to destroy and petrify you. They succeeded. Shaved head, heavy boots and a "poopy" suit (a one-piece jumpsuit). You never took that poopy suit off. Never. Run, eat, swim, sweat, shower, sleep and survive. It was the raunchiest outfit anyone could ever wear. There is no analogy to compare the stench of that poopy.

The day began at 0430 every day with the bugle of reveille. And here's a tip. Should you ever need metal bunk beds, buy them from the Navy-recruit center at Pensacola. Why? And here's the god's truth. They were rarely used! That's right, rarely. The beds were covered and sheeted precisely and to where you probably could have bounced a quarter off of them. But at 0430, you had two minutes to be dressed and out the door for physical training. No time for teeth brushing or bed making. The rooms would be inspected as soon as training and breakfast ended. Breakfast was great food, but you were given only eight minutes to eat while standing. It reminded me of a hog farm and pigs at the trough. The only difference was the smell. The pigs smelled better because they didn't wear poopy suits. Class followed by physical training followed by class, et cetera, throughout the day until 10:00 p.m. (2200 hours). Lights out as we hit the floor for sleep. You wouldn't dare sleep on the bed that would be inspected in six more hours. If your bed wasn't perfect in the morning, drill instructors would crush you with demerits.

Demerits meant marching on a cement quadrangle in noon heat in full gear. Truly hell. So most of us used a rolled-up plastic raincoat for a pillow. I grew to enjoy the floor. Oh no, that's right, nobody liked it. But then there was Sunday. Everyone loved Sunday. It had nothing to do with church and there was no such thing as a day off. But every Monday we were given new linen. Hah, what a joke. The sheets we had were untouched all week. But with new sheets on Monday, we could sleep in our beds Sunday night. Thus the name "hotel night." Run, pushups, swim, climb, be yelled at, screw up every task, an occasional vomit, and there you have it, a Cliff Notes of boot camp. It was definitely one of the most taxing times of my life, but more would follow. Marine drill instructors ran my life for 18 hours of a non-stop day. I would say that the other six hours were mine, but those six hours of sleep were invaded with nightmares of my drill instructor screaming. Actually that was great training for sleeping on an aircraft carrier with planes constantly taking off and landing. There is no real way to describe it. Hell. Two-thirds of my class dropped out. I was too exhausted to quit.

Through it all, there was definitely a bond that occurred. "Help your buddy and someone please help me," was the battle cry. But when the 16 weeks were up, you couldn't help feeling accomplished and proud. You could look at civilians and say to yourself, "Man, if you only knew what I've been through. I truly am one tough mother." I felt so fit and healthy.

It didn't take long to be back at the Cross with John, and my mantra changed to "Pizza, bring it on." John listened kindly to boot camp antics and we slowly worked into the rationale for Vietnam. We both thought it was a crazy war, but I was in a disconnect. Yes,

I was in the military complex, but in my rationalized mind, I was protecting Pensacola. I had nothing to do with the war. Yet!

But the world was becoming more and more real. It was 1967 and my senior year. I had absolutely no interest in school but I now enjoyed weekends at South Weymouth Naval Base because I had been through hell and was now part of the "club." My chief at the Navy base grabbed me one afternoon and listened to my recent "war stories" from Pensacola. He relished seeing a young squid so excited graduating from college in June, and with his recommendation I would be sent back to Pensacola Officer Candidate School. If successful, I would finish as an ensign in the U.S. Navy and proceed to flight school. Christ! Was this really happening? I was absolutely dazzled. An instantaneous "yes" and papers were signed. I had the possibility of becoming a Naval Aircraft Carrier pilot. I walked with a new step and solid posture. I was doing the right thing and would do my best to keep San Francisco safe from communists. Ain't youthful thinking amazing?!

Only one hurdle to overcome. Graduation. Piece of cake. My life to date had been a gauntlet, but what could go wrong here? Well, first, let's put a pinch of tension on the line. In December 1966, six months from graduation, I asked Diane to marry me. She accepted but her parents were dead set against it. Ellen found out about the engagement from Diane's parents and she asked the local priest to refuse to perform the ceremony. A delightful time of arguments and yelling, but to Diane's credit, she was committed. But if I didn't graduate, I'd be an enlisted sailor on a pittance income and orders would be to a swift boat in the Mekong Delta with a life expectancy of 28 days. Okay, I guess I'll graduate. End of problem. Oops, not quite.

So where's the pressure? Wait for it. Here it comes.

In January of 1967, I received a note to please see Father Joe Donahue. Huh? Maybe the Jevies had reconsidered my vocation and they wanted me back. Nah! No chance, but I dutifully met Father Joe in his office. After the usual polite trivial chitchat, I realized I wasn't going to be rebuked. As it turns out, a reprimand would have been easier to take. Father Joe told me that I had a grade point average of 1.98 out of 4.0 and that graduation from Holy Cross required a 2.00. "So I need to get a 2.2 grade point this semester, Father?" "No, Tom, your 1.98 is cumulative for three and a half years. I've done the math and you'll need to take seven courses instead of five and receive two As, three B-pluses, and two Bs." Holy s---! I'd never made a B-plus, much less an A.

Now that's not what I told Father Joe. I said something like "I can do it, Father. Please give me a chance." He agreed to let me take seven courses and I left his office sweating and with shaking knees. What the hell could I do? Alright, it was time for a brain drain. Studying became the name of the game. I was driven to succeed with marriage, enlisted pay, and Vietnam as my everyday core initiatives. And my last semester, which should have been a slide, became a prison of anxiety and tension.

Did I make it? Let's see. Cutting to the chase, I had passed all requirements in all of the courses with only one to go. I needed one more B in Colonial American Literature, a course much akin to castor oil. Disgusting. The night before our exams were due, John and I both had "blue book" exams to take home for these finals. John's test was in a course called Communications. We hated our respective courses equally and had both put in the minimal amount of work throughout the semester. We were doomed, but

John could easily graduate. My chances were slim to none, but we were a team, and better yet, friends. Let's lay it all on the line. John liked historical literature and I was raised in the advertising world where communication was key. Let's take each other's final exams. I swear it was the goofiest, scariest decision ever. John's grade was in my hands but my life was in John's. We spent the night researching each other's material and writing in the blue books. We even tried to copy each other's handwriting. Done. Exhausted. Time for pizza and Cokes. And then the two-day wait for scores. Lots of diarrhea on my part.

Noon, on the Friday before Sunday's graduation ceremony, I received the call from Father Joe. "Congratulations, anchor." Anchor? What the hell did that mean? Anchors aweigh enlisted? Nope. It meant 2.001 GPA. The lowest in the history of the Cross, but I was goddamn graduating! Oh my god. What relief and utter joy. I would be getting married, heading to flight school in Pensacola and saying "See ya" to my best buddy ever, John. Never "Goodbye."

By the way, I got a B-plus score for John and I never let him forget! John scored a measly B for me. He owes me.

But he did pay me back a hundredfold as my true friend. And on more than one occasion, he had exactly the right answer. Once, in particular, his answer changed my life. I remember that I was in my fifties in the mid-1990s and life had painted both of our lives with Life. Careers, children, illness, and all the foibles of living were upon us. My children were grown and gone and I was fully vested in a flourishing surgical practice along with writing and lecturing. As it happens, my wife Diane and I had taken totally different roads. Companionship had long since ebbed and our life together was heading rapidly towards divorce. And as life was in turmoil, I found yoga as a source of calm. Merrill was right there in my classes and love was inevitable. Merrill was in the midst of her own divorce after 20 years. I had been married for 35 years. A lifetime for many. What to do? A life-changing decision. It would affect everyone. Certainly Diane, but also my adult children, and close family friends and relatives. What a mess. And then one Sunday morning after a tearful walk near the Gulf, I decided to call John. I knew that as a devout Catholic he would rebuke me and remind me that divorce and remarrying would mean excommunication from the Catholic Church and the promise of burning in hell. And after explaining my quandary, I asked him, "How can I care for Diane and divorce her because I'm insanely in love with Merrill?" His answer was simple and one I will never forget. He said, "Tom, how can you not?" No more loving and supportive comment has ever been said. And so it would be.

Chapter Nine

Away Aweigh and Away

"Better to be lucky than good"

Graduation day and the wedding to Diane were a blur. And it was not long before we were headed for Pensacola, Florida, and Navy flight training. This must have been a tough time for Diane because her family was very close, or so it seemed. Ellen and Russ, and Chuck and Maggie, the parents of the groom and the bride, were spitefully angry and obstructive. In all fairness, Diane's parents felt that I would die in Vietnam. Disaster for Diane, not to mention me! But off we went. Diane stayed by herself in housing because I wasn't an officer yet. As a cadet, I was ranked slightly above whale dung.

As I walked into the cadet barracks, I was grabbed by a drill instructor (all were called "D.I.") and thrown to floor and yelled at and kicked to pump off 50 pushups. I made it to 20 and collapsed feeling a boot in my butt. There isn't a way to describe the horrors of officer candidate school in 1967. There were no rules for the D.I.s. Kicks, punches, and slaps were all part of the course. The day began again at 4:45 a.m. and always with two hours of physical torture, I mean "training." Academics on aviation aeronautics and naval protocol were the day's curriculum. Then there were the physical challenges meant to drop you from the program. The only analogy that came close was the movie *An Officer and a Gentleman*. It was close but watered down. One of the scenes showed the "Dilbert Dunker." You were strapped in a jet cockpit in full flight gear. The cockpit was 30 feet above a pool and it was released into the pool and crashed. You and the cockpit were flipped upside down and you were expected to release, orient yourself in the bubbles and upside-down mayhem, and make it to the surface. Many of my fellow students went out on this one. Frightening.

The experience of officer candidate school would be a book in itself. You have survived it or it is indescribable. It was an every-hour gauntlet of academics, tests, exhaustion, vomit, weight loss and never-ending fear. The kind of gut-wrenching fear that makes you sick. And yet, in my life as a young cadet, freaks of nature continued to haunt me.

After an eternity of months, one-third of my class and I were pinned as newbie ensigns. Yes, we were officers. And yes, as in the movie *An Officer and a Gentleman* we were saluted by our D.I.s and we handed them a silver dollar. We were suddenly their superiors. No way! A Marine D.I. still scares the poop out of me.

One of the humorous freaks of nature that plagued me happened shortly after becoming a young ensign. The training didn't stop and indeed became more precarious. On one training jaunt, after some training, six of us were flown to 3000 feet and parachuted out into Pensacola Bay. The goal was to hit the water, extract the parachute, inflate your life vest and one-man life raft. The rules were that, once settled, you could not "raft up" and join with your buddies. You were to spend eight hours in your raft getting seasick and dealing with aloneness in the sea. So to make it interesting, my group decided to bet on who could catch the biggest fish to win a cash pool. I was all in!

I was in the water, life vest inflated, in my one-man raft a quarter mile from my closest buddy. Opening the survival pack, I found it filled with absurd junk like "Charms" soft and gooey hard candies and my fishing line, hook, and disgusting gummy worms for bait. A regular scene from *The Old Man and the Sea*. The sun was starting to baste my skin and the saltwater-to-freshwater converter naturally didn't work. I mean, why would it? It was government-purchased from the lowest bidder! That should have told me something about the future. There I was bobbing up and down in sync with the bobber on my fishing line. But not a bite. Whoa! Wait a second. Something's nibbling on the delicious gummies. I yanked up and sure as hell I had hooked one. I'd like to lie and say it was a two-hour battle getting that bruiser into the raft, but truth be told, the fish came in so fast, I think he or she was looking to sunbathe in my raft. Once in the raft, the fish started flapping all over the place and I let my legs dangle out in the water. Six inches of flip-flopping Cap'n D's catch of the day. I finally realized the raft was either mine or Nemo's, so I grabbed the line, cut it and launched my little scaly Moby Dick back to his home in the bay. Whew. Now to relax and enjoy my sunny cruise. Wait a second! Why was my raft filling with water? And air was leaking out. Crap. As I began to submerge, I reinflated my life vest and grabbed one of the two flares I had. Within seconds, the Coast Guard cutter came by and my D.I. was looking down at me. He grabbed the deflated raft but not me. "Looks like you bagged a catfish there, Ensign. Their spine will puncture your raft in no time." Information that came a little too late. Hell, I'm from the Bronx! Ain't no catfish on Webster Avenue there. Catfish, crapfish, I knew only the square fish on the bun at McDonald's. Granted my raft fish wasn't square but no McFish ever came with a freaking spine. "I guess so, Sergeant. Must have been a catfish," I said knowingly. And then in my politest voice, I blurted, "May I please have another raft?" "How's your life vest holding up?" "Fine, thanks, Sarge." (Oops, they hate the nickname "Sarge.") "Good," he said. "Treat it like your lover, son. Where the hell do you think you're gonna get another raft in the South China Sea? Enjoy your swim, sir." And poof, I was alone. I had one flare and my life vest. A big deal? For me it was. It would be four more hours before pickup. My life vest kept slowly deflating. Puff, puff, puff every few minutes to help stay afloat. I held onto my flare like it was Christina Fitzgerald, my fourth-grade love who dropped me like a hot potato as soon as she knew I craved her. But don't you know that the scariest factor was my mind. The movie Jaws wouldn't be out for eight years yet, but every one of us had feared snakes and sharks since we could walk. In my mind, I was dangling in a bouillabaisse of famished sharks. Every wisp of current that brushed by my flimsy flight suit was a Great White in my mind. Four hours of fear, panic, and terror. One good thing was that I could pee to my heart's content. Ah, the small pleasures in life. I've learned to cherish them. But the best joy of all was the Coast Guard pickup boat at 1600 (4:00 p.m.) pulling up next to me. One of my smart-aleck buddies already on board yelled, "Hey, T-bone (my given call sign), where's your fish? Gunny [a great nickname for a Marine drill instructor] said it was a whopper!" I can't remember my reply, but my middle finger was starched straight up. By the way, I was given the name "T-bone" because when I came out of the shower once, my buddies mocked how skinny I was. I stretched out my hands and replied mockingly, "I am the risen Lord." They yelled back that I looked more like a rare T-bone steak in dire need of grilling. The T-bone call sign never left. It still sits on my old flight jacket, 50 years later.

Flight school was grueling from morning until zonk time. I learned to cherish sleep. But even my dreams replayed being in the cockpit with something going wrong. It's been 50 years and I still occasionally wake up in a full-blown sweat. It's always the same. I've ejected but my chute doesn't open and I have to spread my arms like wings to land in a rice paddy. I always wake before skidding onto the rice. When I wake, there's no rice but plenty of water. Then it's into the bathroom and grab a towel to sleep on. There are sure worse things in life to put up with, but damn, it's been 50 freaking years.

Navy flight school is clearly different from all other military branches with the exclusion of the Marine Corps. They trained side by side with us. What makes the Navy program so different? Two words that put the fear of Satan in every flight: "carrier landings." Back then, everyone knew that on one fateful day, they would fly out solo and leave the Navy base. You knew that you'd navigate to an aircraft carrier, the USS *Lexington*, and land on that postage stamp somewhere in the Gulf of Mexico. There would be no instructor in the back seat. Your first landing ever would be solo. It doesn't matter how many movies you've seen, *Top Gun*, *Bridges at Toko-Ri*, there is nothing more frightening than that first carrier "trap." Circling your brain for weeks before that "trap" day, your mind played back every story told about some "nugget" newbie screwing up and "buying the farm" (dying). "Too low, too low! Pull it up, pull it up, for Christ's sake!" The dreaded words from the landing signal officer on the deck watching as you approached the deck. His words, "Wave off, wave off!" were never spoken gently or calmly into your flight helmet. They meant clearly that if you continued, you would crash and die, so add full power and go around. Add to that, if you screwed up enough approaches, you'd be kicked out of the flight program. One fellow in my class had missed two prior approaches and one more would send him back to the base and out. To show how intense it was to succeed, this is what he did. On final approach, he was low again and was ordered to wave off. He knew what that meant, so he pulled the plane's nose up and cut the engine. He missed catching any of the arresting wires that bring you to a stop, but he slammed his brakes and stopped 16 inches from sliding off the bow of the ship. It has never been done again, and by the laws of physics, he should have bought the farm. But he lived. His aircraft survived but I'm sure needed new brakes. The end of the story is that he was dropped from the program. On his release papers, it gave the reason for his dismissal as "No apparent fear of death"!! His release paper still hangs at Pensacola Naval Station. By the way, I finished carrier quals with high marks. No real credit to me. I just happen to have a knack for putting my "bird" (aircraft) in the groove for a deck landing. But after 840 landings on ships in jets, props, and helos, I never walked away from my bird with inside swagger. Sure, the steps and moves were there for all to see, but inside I was always frozen. And maybe that anxious intensity coming aboard actually helped to keep me alive. I always remembered the saying, "There are old pilots and there are bold pilots, but there are no old bold pilots." I understood it. And it has stuck with me in everything I do and not just flying. It kept me and my patients in surgery way out of doo-doo many a time.

Chapter Ten

Vietnam

"What a strange game. The only winning move is not to play"
-War Games

"If red is for hell, then war was in color"
-"The War Was in Color," by Carbon Leaf

There was a burly guy in a gym one day and he was lifting weights that looked like trees. His biceps were bowling balls. He was a friendly enough fellow who sold insurance. He knew of my background and adding it all up he came to the conclusion that I played his ballgame. I didn't. It was an easy mistake. A guy my age with short hair, working out on a rowing machine, with a history of being in the war years before, all pointed to a war hawk and all that went with that title.

It was 2006, and I was knee-deep in healing from some medical catastrophes. He came over and, as he watched the news on TV, he saw our troops in Iraq. "Quite some kicking ass over there, my friend." "I guess so," I replied distantly. He must have picked up my dissonance as he continued, "We want to kick those ragheads' asses, right?" I waited a few seconds and then looked at him and said, "Have you ever been in a war?" "No, I wasn't in the service; why?" A few more seconds passed and I said very solemnly, "I have. And there ain't a smidgen of good in a war or that comes out of a war. I never want to hear the word 'war' again and I sure as hell don't want my children fighting in one. It's 2006, and we're still throwing sticks and stones at one another. Just my opinion, friend." I kept on rowing.

Go to war for only one day, for real, not through the eyes of CNN or Fox News, and I promise it will change your life. One dead child, one fallen buddy. The colors in nature will never be the same. Your anger will never vanish. But I digress.

No, I need to rant about one more aspect of this war and all wars. You don't need to be a Mensa star to realize that war absolutely sucks and represents a bloody display of man's failure to understand and utilize intellect. But here's the thing. After the political leaders and economic gurus have decided to launch our sons and daughters to war, but never themselves, a cascade of horror ensues. Companies make money and politicians can beat their breasts. But in the end, Arlington Cemetery gets bedecked in more white crosses. Know what really boils my blood? Heroes. What heroes? I knew John McCain, and to most he was an American hero. Guess what? I think so, too! But I also think Mike Cappucci from the Bronx was just as much a hero. Mike was an enlisted man serving as a chef in Cam Ranh Bay, Vietnam. He was 19 years old and went from high school to "in country" after boot camp. He left his teary mother, father, and sister for a circus-sized tent outside the airstrip at Cam Ranh Bay. Every morning, Mike woke at reveille and scrambled jillions of eggs and tons of bacon and biscuits for the troops who would shortly pile in for chow. I was lucky enough to have some of Mike's morning chow. But here's the thing. I got to meet Mike because I heard his distinctly Bronx accent. I hit him back with a characteristic, "Hey, muh mahn, ya wahnna piece uv me?" Morning banter that drew from him a s----eating smile. But Mike didn't have a chest of ribbons. Nobody flew the "missing plane" formation or played "Eternal Father" for his family when he was flown home in a flag-draped coffin. Was he a hero? You're goddamned right he was. Every single man and woman who signed up to serve is a hero. Some never went to Vietnam. They stayed in a recruiting booth in Manhattan. So what? The point is that they put their lives on the line each and every day for this country and that's a hero plain and simple. But maybe she never saw combat! Good for her, and lucky for her she never saw battle. Mike served breakfast and died doing it while serving his country. And luck, or kismet, plays a huge part in life. The recruiter could have been the one serving dinner in Cam Ranh Bay, but luck said no. I say thank you, hero. Heroes all.

Why after all these years would I remember an enlisted soldier in Cam Ranh Bay? Freaky, but true serendipity. I had landed in Cam Ranh for aircraft repairs. I loved Cam Ranh because it was far from the war. Three swimming pools (and yes, with lifeguards!), a great officer's club with dancing, great food, and enough liquor to float Vietnam. After a great meal, and way too much Budweiser and Chivas Regal, I made it back to the barracks. Pretty plush for a dormitory-style building. Half was for officers and half for enlisted personnel. I crashed hard on my bunk. Around 3:00 a.m. there was a bright flashlight in my face and a military policeman yelling at me: "Sir, get up and get out of here pronto!" I was still groggy and a bit hung over as I asked, "What the hell is going on?" "Sir, the building has been bombed! You need to be outside in a foxhole!" Crap. Another night without uninterrupted sleep.

When I made it to the foxhole, I was squished with two other Air Force soldiers. I doubt that I said anything intelligible, but I still remember looking at the bombed building through bloodshot eyes. Half of the entire building was destroyed. The North Vietnamese had planted bombs and the bombs worked as ordered. Smoke, debris, and flames remained, but my half of the building was intact. I never heard a thing. Talk about too much to drink. I would have basked in my amazing fortuitous fate, but the joy was interrupted two days later when I asked where Mike was for morning chow. His fate was not fortuitous and he is now on the Wall in D.C. A hero? You bet, every bit of one. The only thing missing was a parade. It's hard to explain the stench of that night and particularly when you know the scent includes human vapors. War just sucks.

That wasn't my only brush with fate. It seems as if my entire life has been woven with threads of serendipity and fate. In fact, a few months after that, two events happened almost freakishly close together.

The first twist happened during a "fun" hop with a buddy I met at the airstrip in Tan Son Nhut just outside of Saigon. First lieutenant Larry Dublin and I hit it off at the "O" club bar at the airstrip. Larry was from Louisiana and had graduated from LSU. I used to jibe him by telling him that the rumor on the street was that LSU would soon be accredited and his diploma might then mean something. I think his retort was something like, "At least I can hack down grits, Mr. Maple Sugar man." He had an afternoon hop in a Phantom and asked if I'd take the back seat. Air Force F-4's, Phantoms, were fitted with flying gear in both seats. The back seat in a Navy Phantom was all decked out for the brains of the operation, the Radar Intercept Officer (RIO). The Air Force version had a throttle and flight stick with full instrumentation. There was always a ton of friendly banter and put-down in the Navy between the pilot and RIO. Actually, to anybody who had the gift of an RIO, the jesting was total camaraderie. A trained RIO located the enemy, targets, the bogeys, and the way back to the carrier. They were chosen back in those days because they didn't have 20/20 vision. But they were pound for pound the brightest. But I would deny ever saying that in an officer's bar, or in any bar for that matter.

The flight was uneventful. Low-level strafing and a tad of napalm. We stayed low at 500 feet heading back to Saigon. Dumb move. Charlie could have thrown up their sandals at us and made a hit. But on this run, it wasn't sandals. Flying over a patch of forest that was designated a No Hit Zone, we were pummeled with small-arms fire. AK-47s were the soup du jour. A high-speed pullup knocked out some of the pings hitting our bird, but we were smoking like a cigar-wielding politician. Number Two engine was out and, although we didn't know it at the time, a lucky slug went through the fuselage and blew the right main gear tire.

Larry called in the emergency and we limped to Saigon at 3,000 feet. The runway was cleared and we had a straight-in approach. Gear down and locked or "three on the green" as we called it. Perfect. Looks like we've made it. Whoosh! Spin! And suddenly we're on the runway like a spinning top. The right tire was out and as the tire strut dragged on the runway, we followed the rules of physics and spun like one of the Globetrotter's trick basketballs. Smoke, plane shaking—maybe a bit less than I—and then sirens and fire trucks surrounded us and foam was hosed on the belly of the bird. The smell of burnt rubber wafted up into the cockpit. Canopy opened and we were out standing on the runway. Larry and I high-fived and swore to toast at the O Club bar. That never happened. I went to my bunk and crashed. I never awakened until the morning sun hit my face. I was still in my flight suit and at least a bit ripe smelling. I know because the "mama san" who came in to clean used international hand-to-nose gestures towards me. Okay, okay, a shower and good ol' Old Spice deodorant. Ready for another day.

But a few days later came another gut-shaker. Even to this day, I can't shake the spookiness of this disaster. Another routine day and my schedule was set. I was fairly experienced at this point, countless months into my tour in Vietnam. The job of maintenance test-flying aircraft fell to me. If a bird had been hit with small arms, damaged, or was just undergoing routine maintenance, it required a flight by an experienced pilot to test its flightworthiness. I was scheduled for an early-morning weather flight to check and report back on any action or untoward weather conditions locally. Then a maintenance-check flight. Easy day. One of my pilot buddies came to me and asked if he could do the weather-check flight and he'd continue the flight westward for support. That way I could do the maintenance-check flight on the aircraft. My buddy was a damned good friend and was soon to leave back for the States. Bernie was a hulky California surfer dude who loved Lucky Strikes and Chivas. Bonded friends. I suggested that he chill for the day and think about his vacation leave coming up. Now as hard as this is to believe, his reasoning was absolutely true. He had 997 hours of flying over Vietnam and if he got to 1000 hours he'd be eligible for the Distinguished Flying Cross. Yup, the same one you've heard was awarded in World War II and Korea for flying involving bravery and heroism. (Oh, that's right, if you flew over Vietnam, in my books you were brave and a hero. You flew a blimp? Great. You make the cut!)

Bernie wanted the Distinguished Flying Cross desperately. I'm not sure why. He was good-looking, had a great personality, and was an easygoing guy. He loved a good time and we certainly had many of those. He was also a great pilot and a sincerely true friend. But all of that wasn't enough to spit on Satan's plans.

I agreed and Bernie took my flight. I flew my maintenance hop and landed to the direst looks of my enlisted aircraft crew. Bernie was dead. His co-pilot Henry was also dead. No, they didn't "pass." We didn't "lose" them. They died. That's the word and there can be no softening of it. Bernie and Henry were shot down in western Vietnam near a small town called Rach Giá. Hours later I jumped into the back of a rescue Huey helicopter to survey the scene. That was the worst mistake I've ever made. It was a brain inlay that would never leave me. The stench and body parts just ate me up. Their aircraft had hit the ground at terminal velocity. That's as fast as possible. Flight boots ripped off, teeth embedded in metal, and, and—that's enough. An angry disgusting sight that can't be described nor should it be. It shook me to my core. But no tears. There wouldn't be tears for a long time away from the war. But what was it running through me? I shook, I poured sweat, I shivered, and I went somewhere in my head that I knew from childhood. A mental hospice with a constant never-ending recording playing the question, "Why not me?" How the hell and why the hell was I spared? Why did I agree with Bernie about the flight change? Was I responsible? There would never be answers to those questions. They still go round and round. Tears? Yes, they came in Phoenix,

Arizona, one year later. I flew to Phoenix and met Bernie's sister. She had his smile, and long hugs and tears followed. We promised to stay in touch but it never happened. Bernie died. No parade, but one hell of a hero, and he'll be in my thoughts until the day I die.

Chapter Eleven

Better to Be Luckier Than Gooder

"A young monk asked the Master about good and evil. The old Master spoke that all men are always battling good versus evil within themselves, like an evil tiger warring with a kind lamb. The young monk asked his elder, 'Who will win?' The Master told him, 'Whichever one I feed'."

So much happens in a war that's decent and heroic, very decent and very heroic. But what's seldom told is that a war unroofs incredible stupidity and unethical evil. Is it because war in itself is so evil? Or is man inherently indecent? Perhaps it comes down to the age-old axiom that we, as human beings, have an ingrained drive to "seek pleasure and avoid pain." I prefer the latter, and, in war, all barriers seem to go down and strip man to the core. The drive becomes "How do I survive, enjoy, get an edge, feel pleasure, and focus on ME?" It becomes a matter of survival and finding those who can give of themselves in such a situation. It is a rare commodity. But let me be more specific.

On a quiet day in the war, on a scorching afternoon with the smell of aviation gasoline fumes mixing with drying fish on bamboo racks, I had literally nothing to do. Humid heat with stench makes me crazy. So I wandered out to the airfield at Tan Son Nhut.

There was a C-117 aircraft being loaded with large cardboard boxes. I would learn later that they were called fifty-fifties. They were filled with cigarettes, candy, toothpaste, coffee, and enough goodies for 50 men for 50 days. (No deodorant, by the way, because the smell could be picked up by the enemy.) These boxes were meant, most particularly, for the outpost troop camps. These were the soldiers living under the most duress, out in the boonies.

The pilot of the C-117, a plane that looked like John Wayne should be flying it, was a workhorse and had been around during the Korean War. The pilot, Lieutenant Commander Gary C., saw my gold wing emblem on my flight suit and asked if I'd like to try a "real" plane without noisy jets. This was a twin-engine propeller bird. Only one possible answer: "You bet." Gary seemed like a "good guy" and was very popular with the enlisted crew. What could go wrong?!

The mission was simple. Fly this hog to outlying airstrips and drop off the fifty-fifties. Great mission, and flying that old antique would be a kick and, as it turned out, tougher than I thought. Balancing two prop engines took some time to control but was a real jolt of fun. Gary was very helpful taking me through the moves of flying that monster and very patient with my initial roughness. Lots of friendly banter between us and with the crew of two in the belly of the aircraft. That, with the smell and look of that plane, gave me a real feel of what historical pilots had to deal with. A real ride through history.

Landing at some of the outlying fields was truly ragged, with dirt runways spitting dust everywhere. And as it settled, we immediately checked the periphery for enemy and any small-arms fire. The troops were an enormous help in that regard, setting up a perimeter around the aircraft. And each stop they showed tremendous gratitude from the troops for the supplies.

Admittedly, I was feeling pretty damned good about the mission and those I was with. The last landing back at Tan Son Nhut was grease, and Gary complimented me profusely. We taxied to the ramp, shut down, and climbed out. But as I was exiting the aircraft, I saw three cardboard boxes in the tail section of the bird, barely noticeable because there were no lights on. But no mistaking it for me, there were three boxes in the aft compartment. And as my flight boots hit the tarmac, I took Gary's arm to get his attention and said, "Commander, we still have three boxes on board. Did we forget a stop?" He pulled his arm away and that told me everything. He was pissed. Briskly he said, "Never mind those, Lieutenant. None of your business. Your flight is over. See ya." Uh-oh, said my gut. I didn't like the way that sounded. I walked to a runway-side Quonset hut and watched as the crew unloaded the three boxes and put them in an approaching Jeep. One of my crew saw me and asked, "What's up, boss?" His name was Jackson and he was a seasoned Chief Petty Officer. He was a no-nonsense guy and dedicated to the Navy and its mission. I explained the day and now the unloading and told him of my smelling something fishy-poo-poo about it. (Okay, maybe not exactly those words.) "I've got it, Lieutenant. I'll track the Jeep and catch you on the back side." "Roger that, Chief, and thanks."

Later that night, there was a knock on the door of my temporary quarters, and the Chief was staring intensely in my doorway.

He explained that the boxes were driven to a warehouse in downtown Saigon and dropped off to a group of Vietnamese men.

Whoa. What the hell was that for? Chief Jackson explained that those fifty-fifties sell for $2500 and are then sold on the black market to the highest bidder and for the wealthy of Saigon. Holy crap, I really didn't want to hear that. What the hell do I do with that information? "Jesus, Chief, this is a mess." The Chief said something like, "It's f------ s---, Lieutenant. You need to hang his ass." "I know, Chief, but you'll probably get involved as well." "No problem, sir."

I was suddenly wrapped up in a quagmire of evil and it was soon to become a big deal. The charges included theft of government equipment and marketeering, netting court-martial and Leavenworth prison time. Why not close my eyes and wake up tomorrow to start a new day and this was a bad dream? I'd be lying if I didn't admit that a few days passed before my diarrhea subsided and I got the gonads to head to the Judge Advocate General in Cam Ranh Bay.

My meeting with the military lawyer was short and sweet. It didn't seem as if he was flabbergasted or thought I was lying. He took it all on tape and made notes, matter-of-factly. He'd be getting back to me and asked that I not mention this to anyone. Roger that.

Two days later things got really crazy. Morning orders came for me to head back to the "Bonnie Dick" aircraft carrier (officially the USS *Bon Homme Richard*), clear my gear, and check into the "in country" town of Hue Phu Bai near the North-South border. It was primarily a Marine base with Navy and Air Force support. It was smack-dab in the boonies. Sweltering tents in mud and dust. It reminds me of the old tent camp in the show *M*A*S*H.* What the hell was going on? Even the ship's yeoman (administrator) couldn't help. All he knew was that I needed to be out of the environment and that I'd be doing a lot of maintenance test flying there. My stateside orders would be to Naval Air Station Patuxent River, Maryland, test-pilot school and naval aircraft testing center. Great orders for a Navy career, but at that point I was thinking my better choice might be truck driver. Anything but more of this life. No more near-misses leading to a fast train to hell for me. But why all the skullduggery of moving me around? Why was I being hidden from my team and crew and now living with Marines?

I checked in with a Marine lieutenant colonel and gave the perfunctory comments about how delighted I was to be in this (hell-hole) command. I was escorted to an officer's tent and settled in. The camp had a really nice group of men and excellent morale in an otherwise tent city bereft of any amenities. Movies were projected onto a bedsheet in the chow hall during the early night to avoid lights exposing where GIs were hanging out. Chow was hardcore but no one seemed to complain. It was definitely not aircraft-carrier cuisine. The "head" (bathroom) was an outhouse-style multi-hole latrine. All this luxury with the addition of 104-degree temperatures with god knows the amount of humidity. Aside from herpes or shingles, what more could you want?

The story of my transfer didn't fully evolve for about a month. Nobody seemed to know anything. Even though I was a "squid" (playful Marine term for a Navy dude), fitting in was a slide. Great guys (yeah, no gals) in a terrible situation. These boys were playing for keeps. I did a lot of maintenance test-flying and took newbies coming into Vietnam for their first flight hops. And every few days a chopper would land and unload a few officers from the JAG corps. Some were from Cam Ranh Bay and occasionally some from Saigon. The lawyer staff was coming to interview me and they were from all branches of the services. Of course, as they brought me into a tent for questioning, the local troops grew suspicious. Was I a criminal? Did they suspect drugs? Every so often, one of the Marines would politely question, "You alright, T-bone?" "Oh yeah, thanks. They're interviewing me for an open slot in the Marine Corps for a gigolo." I'm sure the word "gigolo" was looked up more than once.

The commanding officer of Hue Phu Bai called me to his office one morning and I entered with obvious trepidation. What the hell had I done? He was sitting at his pathetic excuse for a desk with a JAG officer next to him. I remembered the JAG from prior interviews. All in all, a very frightening yet calming meeting. The "hard deck" was that I was being protected in Phu Bai. Protected from what? Well, it turns out that Lieutenant Commander Gary C. had been investigated for black market and drug dealings for a long time. The JAG and NIS (Naval Investigative Service, sort of the FBI for the Navy) were accumulating evidence, and my story along with the Chief's turned out to be the final hammered nail.

Yeah, I understood all that, but what the hell was the protection for? Ever hear of "fragging"? Yes, I had and I sure as hell didn't like the sound of it related to me. Fragging was the term used for the killing of an officer by an enlisted man. The intent was to get rid of the officer and have the killing look as if it were committed by the enemy. Christ! Who would want that done to me?

It turns out that Gary had a small army of enlisted men who were well paid to do his bidding. Gary would be returned to the States for prosecution, but his army of accomplices was unknown and now the golden goose had been shut down—by me! The NIS was very direct in stating that the "army" was in Saigon and retribution would be unlikely, but better safe than sorry. My depositions would suffice, so I wouldn't have to face Gary at his court-martial. A small but much appreciated gift to me. I never heard what happened to Gary and I was never contacted again about it. And of course I was reminded that the least said the better. No problem with that order, sir!

Life became immensely better now that I knew what was happening and why it had happened. I settled into a daily routine of paperwork, troop inspections and maintenance flight checks. Even the chow started to taste—well, filling. It sure didn't get me running for the chow bell. Of all the things I remember, their burgers (sliders) were identical to the White Castle burgers I knew from my time in the Bronx. I'm not sure what was in those burgers, but damn, they tasted delicious and they were soaked in smothering chopped onions. Why do we remember such small absurd moments in our lives? I have no clue.

Now the game plan was surviving. Stay alive to make the flight back to the States in a few weeks. Except for the proximity to the North-South border and "incoming rockets" to the camp at night, my life would be pretty much routine. Oh, that's right. I've never had the pleasure of "routine." And shortly, routine would fall apart again.

It was a gorgeous Sunday afternoon and the chaplain was finishing Mass. I had a pang of guilt for not attending. The pang didn't last long. The executive officer of the base came into my tent and I snapped to attention. His nickname was "Woody" and he was not an aviator, but one hell of a great guy. As a junior officer, though,

I would never call him Woody. He was "Yes, sir," and "No, sir" to me. As a Marine major, he was right off the shelf from Macy's. Trim and fit to a fault, his fatigue uniforms were immaculate. I swear that the man didn't have a sweat gland in his body. But as I said, he was a wonderfully intelligent and just leader.

After the usual small talk and niceties, Woody said, "Tom, I have a request for you." (Notice, not an order.) "Yes, Sir," was the only appropriate answer. The request was a simple flight that afternoon to test-fly a helo with a newbie young Marine, new to the base and Vietnam. If the bird checked out, I would continue the flight down to Da Nang to pick up Claymore mines and return them to the base. For me, that sounded like a piece-of-cake mission and one that the XO would really appreciate. It was even more palatable because it was Sunday. This will sound strange, but most military ops quieted down on Sunday. Sure the war was still going on, but far fewer flights were scheduled. It was a relative day for kicking back and having a beer. It was time to fly.

There was an enlisted man in the camp who didn't get to do or see much. His nickname was "Ecky." He was one of those amazing young guys who enlisted in the Navy to "serve his country." He probably felt it was his duty to keep the "commies" away from the U.S. coastline. He wasn't alone in that belief, as silly as it sounds. But Ecky's job in Phu Bai was to keep aircraft data for flights that happened each day. Essentially, he lived in a Quonset hut and transcribed numbers. Good god, how boring for someone keeping our U.S. coastline safe! Ecky was always in a good mood and smiling at every moment. But like so many in his predicament, how do you write home and explain to Mom and Dad what you were doing? They were sitting at home watching Walter Cronkite list the number killed that day and they were petrified for their son. Meanwhile, he was getting finger fatigue at his air-conditioned desk. Well, Ecky came up with an answer. One day he put on his combat fatigues, which had never been worn, and he borrowed his bunkmate's M-16 rifle and helmet. Then he trekked out to the "shit lake" behind the aircraft. This was a ditch that captured the oil, gas, and filth from the aircraft after they were hosed down. So Ecky jumped in and smeared the goo on his face and fatigues. Then he posed as if he was climbing out of the ditch, but he was looking away from the camera that his bunkmate was holding. It looked like he was scouting for the enemy. The picture was a classic and could have made it as a front cover of *Time* magazine.

Ecky sent the picture home to his parents and to his Baptist church pastor. Results? You bet. Ecky had a stream of cookies, cakes, doughnuts, and crackers by the truckload. The joke of the day was that as you brought your flight record to Ecky, you'd ask, "What's the pogey bait of the day?" "Pogey bait" was GI slang for goodies and junk food. Ecky loved it and he was more than generous giving out the riches to everyone. Ecky had a heart as big as his pogey bait closet.

I met the newbie whose name was Buck Dillard, from West Virginia. Buck was my six feet two inches in height but weighed in at 250. He was a tree, and our meeting went something like a version of *The Beverly Hillbillies* show. So, Buck, that's an interesting name. Family name? And in the best accent of a West Virginian hillbilly he told me, "Mah great-great-grandaddy was a 'Buck' and mah grandaddy was a 'Buck' and mah daddy was a 'Buck' and 'course I'm a 'Buck'." And then he showed me a huge country grin. You gotta love him. This guy was a down-to-earth, rock-solid good guy. He had the kind of demeanor that spoke, "I'll back you anytime and I'm as honest as ol' Abe." We bonded instantly. I loved putting on my worst hillbilly accent when I spoke to him. He'd laugh and tell me I sucked and that he'd never take me home to meet his "mahmaw" and daddy. I lost touch with Buck after the war, as I did with almost all those I flew with. In my later years I've come to understand why I never stayed close. I realized with the help of my "shrink" that I didn't want to risk any more losses. I had been taught not to show my emotions, but the hurt was very deep. Admittedly, even now, in the dark of night when the house is asleep, I can sit by myself and just belly-ache cry. Sounds a tad nuts, but I always feel better and sleep the rest of the night in peace.

"Excuse me, Lieutenant, but I was wondering if I could go on the hop with you?"

It was Ecky all decked out in flight gear, blond hair blowing from the aircraft exhaust.

"Ecky, we'll be flying over no-man's land and you could get hurt. You also don't have flight status on your orders. You can't joyride anytime you like."

"Sir, there's a box of Entenmann's chocolate chips riding on this flight. Please, sir, I really need this."

Hell, it was Sunday, low probability of trouble; okay, why not? You'd have thought Santa had brought this South Carolina native a pony for Christmas. And naturally, his camera was loaded for bear. I wondered how many cupcakes those pictures would bring in. The helo checked out so I picked up the crew and filed for Da Nang.

Loaded, cranked, and clearance from the tower to launch, and we were airborne. Ecky couldn't keep from giggling nonstop. The gun bay on the helo was manned by a Marine gunner who was not in the mood for Ecky's shenanigans. He kept pushing Ecky back into the helo telling him that he didn't want Ecky falling out, although they were both strapped in. The noise from the engine and rotors overhead was deafening but that didn't slow down Ecky. All in all, it was a fun flight to Da Nang with no incidents.

We landed in Da Nang at two-ish and taxied to the hangar to load the "mines" on board the aircraft. All of us chowed down on box lunches we brought from Phu Bai. Bologna on white bread with cheddar cheese, soda, and an apple. Mmm!

Loaded to return to Phu Bai, we took off heading north. I climbed to 3,000 feet just to be safe or safer. I gave Jerry the "stick" or control of the aircraft as I settled back and watched Vietnam pass rapidly underneath. I was very comfortable and Jerry seemed to have great control of the aircraft. Now, you never really relax in combat, but I was pretty comfortable. Ecky was a photo maestro down below and having a ball.

BLAM! The helo shook uncontrollably and the cockpit and bay of the aircraft filled with smoke. I couldn't see much but I did see flames surrounding the aircraft. I quickly called in a mayday and gave our coordinates. Jerry was shaking, and I grabbed the stick and collective, yelling into the mic, "I got it!" I shut the engines immediately and hoped that would quell the fire. It didn't. Then I auto-rotated the helo. That's essentially disconnecting the rotors from the engine, making it a basic pinwheel, like the one children play with. But I was no child and this was no game. We were heading into a rice paddy. Air Center called for a repeat of the coordinates and Jerry fired them back quickly and accurately. His voice sounded a bit like Mickey Mouse's, but damn, there was no one in that aircraft that wasn't radically terrified. This was my third shootdown but I was filled with havoc. I had lost my Mickey Mouse panic voice as I radioed below for the crew to prepare for a crash. We'd been hit by a 50-caliber machine gun. That's a huge ground weapon and it fires a bullet that doesn't have your name on it. Carved in the casing, it says, "To Whom It May Concern."

Windows open, fuel off, and looking for a spot to land in the rapidly approaching rice field. The thing about an auto-rotation was that you get only one chance. Your rotors have been pinwheeling and building up energy. Then, just before landing, you could raise the collective. That would change the pitch of the rotors and turn that massive set of rotors into a parachute effect. But as you bleed off that energy on the rotors to soften the landing, there's no way to get it back. Apply the parachute effect too high, and you'd drop like a rock. It will ruin your whole day. On the other hand, too late a parachute effect and you'll be crashing into your coffin. Just right. You have to hit it just right.

This was especially tough because I couldn't see the ground. Partly obscured by the smoke in the cockpit, the solid ground was covered with Mama's rice pudding. Water, water everywhere, but how deep down was terra firma?

I stuck to my old mantra of "aviate, navigate, and communicate." I have no idea if anyone was talking to me. I was hell-bent on flying that bird into the paddy. And so I did. As the Skeds and ground braces touched the water, I pulled collective and gently lowered us into the mud pond. Down down down we sank. I wondered if this was quicksand or if I had found the hole through the earth. Jeezuz, when would we touch down? There! The left mount stopped and felt solid. Whew! What a relief. Wait a damned second. Something was wrong. It was a perfect auto-rotation. In the

Olympics I would have given myself a nine point nine. But no gold ribbon today, of course. No "routine" in my life. I noticed that the right-sided mount continued to sink and the aircraft tilted right. I had landed on a small underwater cliff. Whop-whop, the rotors hit the water and the aircraft lurched like a bucking bronco. In an instant we were all tossed around, and when the shaking stopped, I yelled "Abandon ship." I probably should have said to abandon the aircraft, but at that moment I was struggling to find my Clint Eastwood voice.

The crew was out in a New York second. Jerry was next, and then I climbed/jumped out. From the angle of the now-deceased helicopter, looking much like one of Kit Carson's dead buffaloes, my fall was high. I remember catching my right knee and flight suit on part of the helo, and it tore open and scraped the joint. Bleeding was minor, but the bruise still tries to come back today from time to time.

The crew gathered around the bird and everyone crouched down in the paddy. We all had our handguns unlocked and loaded, and scoured the horizon for Charlie. He was nowhere to be seen. And neither was Ecky, for that matter! I yelled for him and my gunner called to me that he was aft of the chopper ten yards. I looked and spotted him waist-deep in the rice paddy, but he was taking off his flight suit only to expose his white undershirt. On the one hand I was very proud of him. I thought he was setting up a perimeter. But he hadn't been taught any combat maneuvers. I signaled for him to squat down. If Charlie was watching, Ecky probably looked the way a poster of Marilyn Monroe looks to prison inmates. But dutifully, Ecky took the squat.

Whop-whop-whop, the most delicious sound you could ever hear in that situation. Rescue helicopters. One was a Huey from HAL-3, an attack squadron, and the other was a dustoff Huey, an air ambulance for rescue in Vietnam. They had heard our mayday.

Ecky came plodding towards us. As we climbed aboard, Ecky's combat brilliance came into view. He wasn't setting up a perimeter. His flight suit was now off and his skivvies were showing. The flight suit and the back of his skivvies were covered in diarrhea. Ecky had actually been "scared s---less."

The rescue helicopters headed to Saigon for all of us to be checked out by Army doctors stationed at Tan Son Nhut. The plan was to reconvene after being cleared and head into Saigon for some well-deserved R and R (rest and recuperation). I was more than ready, and after checking that we were all good to go, we left the screening room at the hospital. Hold on a second. They all headed to downtown Saigon, but Tommy boy didn't go. My knee was cleaned and bandaged and I thought I was fine. A lovely nurse stopped me and asked me to wait for the doctor. The crew said they'd wait, but the nurse told them that I wouldn't be leaving that night. They figured it was my knee. But shortly after the crew left, a young Army doctor came in and started asking me questions about nausea, fevers, change in my bowels, fatigue.

Well, truth be told, I had a touch of all those, but hell, who in Vietnam didn't have them? "What's the problem, Doc?" He was very matter-of-fact and looked me in the eye saying, "Lieutenant, your blood test shows you have malaria. You'll be here a few days to determine what phase you're in and we'll start you on a medicine called chloroquine. It has excellent results, but you'll need to be followed when you get back to the States." Great! No drinking and lots of blood tests with some medicine I can't pronounce. I was getting really pissed with this whole Vietnam thing and how my life seemed like a magnet for disasters. I called the XO to update him and he was already in the know. A friendly, "Just get well and holler for a pickup." They had already launched two A-4s off the *Enterprise* to scuttle the downed chopper. It must have made a great ka-boom with those Claymore mines on board. Nothing left for Charlie to pick over. I would have loved to have seen that pie in the sky, but enough excitement for one day. Into the hospital bed for three days with an I.V.

And here are the takeaways from that skirmish. First, the crew had a ball in downtown Saigon and the XO granted them 48 hours' liberty. Saigon will never be the same. But I heard on the best authority, my door gunner, that no one ever said a single word, joked about, or smirked to Ecky about his chocolate pants. No one. I'm sure they all thought, "That could have been me!" I sure felt that way.

And when I left "in country," Ecky was there to send me off. He told me often, "Thanks for saving my life, Lieutenant." I told him often and honestly that I was as frightened as the rest and I probably would have stepped on his back to get out myself. He just never bought it. Much as I tried to run from Vietnam vets, I couldn't shake him. Wherever I went in my life after the war, Ecky found me and called. And get this: Every winter he sent Diane, my ex-wife, a dozen roses. "With love from Ecky. Remembering when T-bone saved my life." Ecky left the Navy and went on to become a very successful businessman in South Carolina. He still calls. I still listen. I still want the Entenmann's chocolate-chip cookies.

Chapter Twelve

You Can Run But You Cannot Hide—From You! If You Think You Can or You Think You Can't—You're Right!

Did you ever want something so badly day after day that your blood was effervescent? For me, it was a Stallion 45 cap pistol when I was nine years old. It was so real-looking, had a holster, and was identical to the one Hopalong Cassidy used in his cowboy TV series. Christmas couldn't arrive fast enough. And then it happened. Christmas Day and that Stallion 45 was strapped around my pajamas from underneath the tree. Later, Ellen and Russ had a few cocktails and the yelling had begun. Weeks of exciting expectation vanished like Houdini's rabbit. My cap pistol became obsolete overnight and something to stare at and take in. That was just like my departure from Vietnam and return to the States.

There was no marching band or relatives galore to meet me. I landed in California as if it were Mars. So much had happened in 15 months and I couldn't take it all in. I would have three days of I.V. medications and then three months of pills to take for the malaria. In the hospital I was warned that, if I planned on taking a walk into town when not on the I.V., it would be best not to wear my uniforms. My corpsman proceeded to explain that most Americans hated the military. "Make love, not war," was the slogan of the day. I was reminded of a reply from a World War II vet: "Hell, back in '45, we did both!"

Kennedy had been assassinated, some guy named "Tricky Dick" Nixon was president, protesters were everywhere, and fast food was on every block. What happened to all the green jungle, scorching heat, and explosions? Who were all these young women in short shorts and tie-dyed muumuus? And why the hell were they giving me the look? Khaki trousers, blue button-down shirt, and spit-shined loafers. How did they know I was military? Oh yeah! Everyone else was in torn blue jeans and the longest hair I'd ever seen. God, I was close to bald in comparison. Military tight bald. Wasn't I special-looking? I was called "pig" a few times and once, "killer." Yup, I was sure glad to be home. A real warm and comfy feeling filled my bones. Not!

When I went for a drink and smoke, I went alone. I didn't want to talk 'Nam with other GIs and sure as hell didn't want a Socratic debate with a hippity-dippity doo-dah. Didn't they know that the reason they could rant and rave in the streets was because soldiers were dying for that freedom? Yes, I actually said that to myself. I was the good guy and they were the enemy, but there were a hell of a lot of them. It would be years before I realized how insane the war, or any war, really was. Want to end all wars? Let the warring countries' leaders get naked and duke it out for all to see. Guarantee: no more wars.

It was time to be a recluse and that's exactly what I became. Daily phone calls to my wife Diane let her know I was fine and would be heading to the East Coast shortly. Yes, I was very excited to see her and head to our new duty station at Patuxent River's test center. Truthfully, I was in a stupor and words dribbled out. My thoughts were always backtracking to Vietnam and those that I had left behind and those who would never return. And then I'd see young adults living it up and with disdain for me. Silently I would yell to myself, "You pukes have no idea about life, death or war. Not a freaking clue. Just have another joint and some 'suds' while life rolls on." Damn, I was truly pissed. And that anger wouldn't subside easily or quickly. My world was a jumble of turmoil and emotion and no one to talk to about any of it. Diane had been on the front page of a local paper in the midst of a group of angry protesters. Christ! I had no place to run from my mind. I wouldn't realize until years later that the protesters were a major cause for us to leave the war. But back then they were like spit in my face. A reminder of how lost I was and how I didn't fit in anywhere.

Arriving in New York's LaGuardia Airport was another wake-up into a land of horror shows. Hot, sticky, and humid, with more people than I had seen in quite a while. And smells! Tons of mixed scents: flower shops, McDonald's French fries, pizza, Chinese food kiosks, and of course alcohol and cigarettes. A regular haven of healthy living to come back to.

I met Diane in the city and we spent the night at the Waldorf Astoria. It was great to see her again, but I'd be lying if I said a bond of comfort existed between us. "How are you? How are you feeling? You've lost so much weight! Do you want something to eat?" All kind of inquiries and a nervous demeanor on her part that said exactly what I was thinking: "I don't know what to say or do." Two people meeting as if for the first time. Now I really didn't fit in, and that became incredibly apparent the next day.

We left the Waldorf (and holy crap, did that wipe out the checkbook. I hadn't paid for a thing for a year and a half) and took the New Haven train to Larchmont, in Westchester County. Westchester was known for its wealthy inhabitants and flamboyant homes on the Long Island Sound. My parents lived in one of those exuberant homes, now that my father had climbed the advertising staircase to the top. Diane's parents lived on the other end of town in an even more lavish estate. They had eight children and tons of money. The house was run by Chuck, the father, and Maggie, the mom. They lived an extremely Catholic strict religious lifestyle and all the kids lived in dread of the "old man." He had the purse strings and he had the drunken anger. His passions were money, stocks, and sailing at the yacht club. Diane was his shining daughter who could do no wrong, other than date me.

It had all been arranged. Dinner at five preceded by cocktails galore. The dinner was a raw prime rib that I couldn't even fake swallowing. I fell back on an old childhood trick of covering the "yuckies" with mashed potatoes. I remember watching the meal and staring at the trembling kids and drunk parents. This wasn't going to end well. I could feel it in my gut. Shortly after dinner, Chuck lit up a Lucky Strike and, taking my arm, escorted me into his den. The den was a typical elitist man cave adorned with diplomas, business awards, and sailing trophies. He had a huge wooden desk and red leather chairs placed in front of the desk throne. There was a giant globe of the world, made to look antique, and a glass-topped coffee table. How do I recall all of that? Here's why.

Chuck started with some nicety chit-chat and then went right to the core. He stood in front of the coffee table and what seemed like an inch from my face. The bourbon was pungent, mixing with the cigarette stench. It took him no time to get his point across. He started trying to intimidate me by saying, "I bet you think you're some kind of hot shit now that you're a pilot and back from the war!" I said nothing but I felt my rage soaring. "I want every one of your goddamned bills and I'm taking an insurance policy out on your ass so when you kill yourself flying, my daughter will be taken care of." I was seething. And then he took his index finger and rammed it into my throat saying, "And I want this done now!" I would have been fine if he hadn't touched me. The proverbial last straw, and call me a camel. I took my fist and threw it into his chest. You can guess the rest, but it basically tossed Chuck back onto the coffee table, breaking the glass. I would have loved to have had some cool moves and words at that moment, but truth be told, I was shaking like a leaf. I blurted out something like, "Get up, m-----f-----, and I'll kill you!" Unfortunately, most of his kids had heard the battle, along with Diane and Maggie. Not a word was spoken, and no one ran to check on dear old Dad. I took Diane back to her car and headed back to the Waldorf. Diane was crying and I doubt I said anything other than "I'm sorry." I wasn't.

My relationship with Chuck never did get any better over the years. We never spoke and his only other contact from me came four or five years later. I was stationed at Bethesda Naval Hospital and Diane had taken our son Mark home to see the family. She called sobbing one evening and explained that Chuck had taken Mark by the neck and forced him to kneel in front of some home religious shrine. He was yelling at Mark that, by god, if his parents weren't teaching him to pray, his grandfather would show him the way to heaven. Was it the time, the war anger, my childhood? I don't know and I don't care. I was out-of-control nuts with anger. Fortunately

I couldn't get off base because I was "on call." I was packed and had my .45 locked and loaded. But that wasn't gonna happen. The Shore Patrol wouldn't let me off base and there was no one to cover for me. But I was so enraged I'm not sure what I would have done. What I did was write a scathing letter to Chuck. I explained the gun and how I wanted to annihilate him. He would drink this episode away, but I never would. I went on to tell him that he was less than whale feces to me and that until his death he should know that I knew him to be far less than a man. And that anytime I would see him, he'd know that was exactly what I was thinking. I don't think I ever saw him again, though. He went sailing one day and came home to rest and died in his bed. The whole relationship with him was a constant reminder of the question: Were all families as screwed up as mine? I gave up alcohol the night I wrote the letter. I would take no chances with my family.

Diane and I headed south to Patuxent River Naval Air Station. The entire way I felt as if I were having an enema. Get me away from everybody and everything. Before I left Larchmont, though, I did stop by and say goodbye to Ellen and Russ. It didn't take but a second, but it was pleasant compared to what I had left at Diane's house. Russ wanted to know all about flying and 'Nam. Ellen listened and made small talk with Diane. Russ had a thousand questions and I probably answered two of them. I felt a smidge of sadness for Russ because this is what he had dreamed about. He had studied and designed rockets as a young boy. He saw a Goddard rocket launched from Massachusetts and had Goddard's autograph. He joined the Army Air Corps during World War II in the hopes of flying but, as mentioned, he was rejected from flying because he was too thin. He spent his time during the war teaching at the

War College, in Carlisle, Pennsylvania. I don't think he ever got over that loss. A brilliant man, he went on to become the president of McCann-Erickson Advertising. For him, tons of money, tons of fame, but it wasn't the same as landing on board an aircraft carrier.

Patuxent River, Maryland, was an out-of-the-way lost town near the Eastern Shore of Maryland. Naval test flying was studied and performed there and still is, for that matter. Back then, the town had the base, 18 bars and diners, and a 31 Flavors Ice Cream store. Diane actually worked at the ice cream store and she loved it. It became an outlet for her obsessive-compulsive disorder. She wouldn't leave the store until it was immaculate. It was great for her because my schedule was hectic with academics and flying. My class wouldn't actually start for months but I had mandatory classes and I was assigned as the maintenance test pilot for the base aircraft.

We had a great apartment in a farmhouse on the St. Marys River. Great sailing and so peaceful. The calm was intermittently shattered by the sound of the afterburner of a Navy jet tooling overhead. It was certainly a chance to try and flush Vietnam out of my mind. But the image of children strewn and scorched on the ground near their huts made me belly-sob. All of the horror during my tour was somewhat shelved under "the disgrace and carnage of war." I mean, that's what I'd been taught. John Wayne didn't cry and, after all, we were the good guys saving America. Try telling that to me now as an old geezer looking back. What stands out most are the children. God, the children. Please don't tell me there's honor in war. Sorry, but like herpes, the images keep coming back even now.

Patuxent River was placid and a far cry from what I'd left. Perhaps the momentary calm at Pax River focused my mind on what I would do with the rest of my life. (Interestingly, *pax* in

Latin means "peace.") Change doesn't come easily to any of us, and it was a struggle for me. I wanted some calm. I did know, however, that my next tour out of Pax would be another aircraft carrier and more deployments. Diane and I wanted children, but that was to be another mud slide. Diane had multiple pregnancies and all terminated in miscarriages. The topic became so painful that we decided we couldn't have our own children and the subject was closed. I was crushed, but Diane handled it like hearing "no dessert tonight after dinner." The multiple miscarriages probably eased the loss of future expectations. Life fell into a humdrum routine. But not for me. What would I do with my life? I'd had too much Jesuit training in philosophy for me to come up with "Que será será."

Teaching became a more than distinct possibility. Flying with the airlines came in a close second. I signed with TWA for one dollar a year. It guaranteed me a spot with the company when I left the military and the time would count for seniority. But more and more I was remembering my combat tour and I was losing the lust for aviation. What about medicine? I loved the thought, but had graduated last in my college class and I thought "cell biology" was spelled "sell biology." How could I catch up with all the science requirements? And then two episodes happened at Pax that helped direct me.

It all started with a quiet Saturday morning when I was the duty officer for the weekend. I was on call for any flight emergencies or problems on the base. That would mean sleeping on the base and having Diane come in for a fast-food diner meal we'd share in the duty officer's space overlooking the runways. I'd had this duty many times before and for the most part it was a perfunctory boring weekend. On this particular day, "boring" flipped in a New York heartbeat. It started with a benign phone request from the XO of the base. He informed me that a retired admiral was dying at Johns Hopkins hospital in Baltimore, Maryland. His request was to die on his family's island, Smith Island, in the Potomac River off the coast from Patuxent River. I was to take a new station pilot, Tony Medusa, as a co-pilot in the base helicopter and transport the Admiral. No problem. A light flight up the coast. What could be better?

I met Tony at the helo and he was actually more familiar with the base and the area than I. He was a really nice fellow, set to leave the service as a marine aviator and fly for the airlines. He had tons of helicopter flight time.

We launched up the coast and I was essentially a passenger. Tony was the plane commander and he loved to fly. We had a Navy corpsman in the belly of the helo to care for the admiral on the way to Smith Island. Routine, perfect, a real walk in the park.

As we approached Baltimore, the sky exploded with lightning, clouds, and horrific rain. No problem. And then most of the instrument lights in the cockpit went out. Most of the flight had been learning about Tony's life and family, so a small emergency only sparked some excitement, but no sweat really. But as the clouds closed in, the situation became serious. No navigation equipment to find the hospital. Communication was static at best when we tried to get directions to the hospital. "Lower your altitude and look for a building with a roof in the shape of a cross." That would be the Baltimore V.A., and the admiral would be there. For fun, fly over Baltimore someday. Every other building has a roof in the shape of a cross! Oh, there's one with a large field behind it. Tony started our descent through fog and clouds. We broke out of the scud and realized we were landing in a dump. Yup, a dump. Cans, papers, old towels, and the kitchen sink all went flying. Kids ran out of the surrounding tenements and approached. The corpsman waved them off but they wanted a ride. I told Tony let's speed launch straight up unless he wanted to adopt four or five of these kids. In a second, we were launched and again, cans and banana peels went flying. God only knows if any of it hit the kids.

Now, flying low and in the fog, I was getting a tad anxious. Where the hell were we and where do we go? Our corpsman had an FM radio and contacted the Maryland police. "No problem, Navy; just follow our flashing lights to a lit field straight ahead. We'll divert your passenger to the field." And sure enough, bang, there was a field coming into view and Tony set up to land. We approached lower and lower and broke through the fog. We landed. Oops, it was Baltimore Memorial Stadium and we were setting down on first base. Good lord, what a mess. The police started to divert the admiral to first base. The stands continued to fill with game spectators. What an embarrassing disaster, but sure enough the admiral was gurneyed to the helo and he got a standing ovation from the crowd.

Ready to launch and call it a day. Almost. Tony looked at our spot on the field and realized with the fog present we couldn't lift up and launch. I decided to tell him a technique that would work. "Go for it!" he said. We both wanted out of this predicament. The maneuver is a high-speed pullup. You fly just above the ground picking up airspeed, and then, as you approach the upcoming obstacle, you yank on the stick and pull "G's" for sudden aggressive altitude. And that's what I did. We made it out of the stadium to the unheard but seen applause of the fans.

Whew! Now heading to Smith Island where the admiral's family was eagerly waiting. And then came the call from the corpsman: "Sir, I think we lost the admiral. He has no vital signs and he's bleach white and unresponsive." Holy crap. The admiral is dead! Now here's the question. Did the high-speed pullup do it? Or was he brought to us deceased? We'll never know. We flew him to his family and medical team on Smith Island and never heard another word. Ever. Sometimes when I remember that flight, I completely rationalize and tell myself that if I'm 94 and dying, I'll take a high-speed pullup anytime.

Almost no consequences from that—except one. Channel Four news videotaped the entire escapade. We were met at Pax by the Shore Police who escorted us to the XO. There were no kind words. There were no commendations. Just a brisk, angry "Dismissed!" We did make the evening news and I still proudly keep the videotape of that high-speed pullup. I wonder if Tony ever used that technique at Delta, where he later became their chief pilot.

By now, the glamour of flying was rapidly draining. But wait, this is Tom. I would need more and, like the answer to a prayer, more was right around the corner.

In the summer months at Patuxent River, there was an unspoken tradition on the base. It was an unspoken tradition because the activity was strictly against Navy rules. Nonetheless, the adage "act now and ask forgiveness later" was the word of the day. So on Thursdays, the wives and crews on the base would go door-to-door taking orders for Maine lobsters, crabs, and clams. It was like the opening day of a Target store sale. The order was called in and the pickup flight scheduled. Needless to say, it was a plane full of fresh seafood. What could possibly go wrong?

On one particular Friday, I was chosen co-pilot to fly with a seasoned commander to Brunswick, Maine, to pick up the seafood order. The prices were so inexpensive we could have serviced the entire East Coast. The aircraft was an S2F, a twin-engine prop mini-cargo plane. It was used to bring items and passengers on and off an aircraft carrier and was called the C.O.D. (carrier onboard delivery).

It was a great day for flying and I felt as if this might reinstate me with the higher-ups after the high-speed pullup debacle. Perfect flight up the coast and in time for a lunch of lobster rolls at Mindy's in Brunswick, just outside the gate. The plane was loaded while we loaded ourselves with delicious fresh lobster on a bun. Now this was the Navy! This was what I had signed up for.

At 1400 (2:00 p.m.), takeoff, and bellies were full. I do remember that the aircraft had a pungent "fishy" smell. All of the lobsters were alive and packed in soaked seaweed. Ceiling and visibility unlimited as we flew back to Patuxent River. Hell, maybe the commanding officer would give us a medal for the snappers we were bringing back for everyone.

We set for landing at Patuxent at around 1900 (7:00 p.m.) and the weather was still in our favor. Landing checklist run-through, and we were set. Almost. There are three little green lights that show up when you land that indicate your three landing gears are down and locked. It goes without saying, that's a good thing to have if you're landing. Two greens and a red light just won't make your day and yet, there they were, staring at us. Our nose gear was red. Not locking and engaged. Crap. We did a flyby past the air-traffic tower to confirm, and the controller looked and confirmed that the nose gear was hung up. We climbed to altitude and yanked up hard on yoke to pull Gs and hopefully loosen the gear. No luck. Hand crank wouldn't release it either. Hmm, is this what you get when you buy from a company that's the lowest bidder on aircraft?

Okay, we had a carrier arresting hook, and the base had a runway with a retaining wire for this sort of calamity. The commander took control and set up for an emergency landing. The fire and foam trucks were ready and waiting. It was a nice approach, but with only one wire, no room for error. I had learned to hate that phrase, "no room for error." And sure enough, we erred. Missed the wire, cut the engines, and slammed into the runway. Sparks, smoke, fumes. I had been in this rugby match before. Foam and water everywhere as we left the aircraft. No injuries, or, should I qualify, no human injuries. Lobster and crab salad with foam and hose water saturated the aircraft. Half of the base watched as their Friday night dinner was ruined. I did hear later that many went through the rubble when clear and pulled out their bounty. But as they say, if the commanding officer ain't happy, ain't no one happy. I had to go through an accident investigation board, but the commander was the PIC (pilot in command) and thus took the heat. I merely corroborated what a great job he did trying to save the aircraft. I'm not sure what that cost him in future ranks. I flew the last Brunswick seafood flight, and that was it. Quite an honor, if I do say so myself. Oh, the plane? Totaled. A complete loss. Not from the nose mount failure and underbelly damage. Nope. From the stench of fish. There was no way to eradicate the putrid odor. And to this day, I rarely order lobster for dinner.

Chapter Thirteen

Catching the Three Wire

"Two roads diverged . . ."

That last fiasco on the lobster run might have been the turning point. I mean, I was already wondering where my life was headed but I sure as hell didn't want it to end in a heap of crunched metal. I had been amazingly lucky, but luck doesn't last forever.

I spent lots of time talking to Diane about the possibility of going to medical school and she agreed for me to give it a shot. So I took a day and went to D.C. and spoke with the dean of Georgetown University School of Medicine. He listened to my story and it probably took all of his effort not to tell me to look into truck driving. I had no science background, had graduated as the anchor from college, and was ten years over their age for acceptance. (Times have changed.) His actual words were that the odds of getting in *if* I aced all the science courses and maxed the entrance exam would be one in a thousand. He apologized to me for his facts, but that was the medical criteria then. Georgetown had 13,500 applicants and accepted 120 students. "Please let me know if I can be of any other help. And thank you for your service." Words I have grown to despise, even today.

WWGD? (What Would Granny Do?) I wasn't sure, but I had a feeling it would have gone something like, "Kick their butts, Sonny, and get in!" And so the decision was made: medicine. Diane must have thought I was nuts, but every night after work, I would take pre-med courses and prep courses for the MCAT entrance test.

A year later I was applying to schools. And almost immediately I was granted an interview at Harvard. Harvard! Jeez, how hard is this med school thing? They want me! What could go wrong? I put on my pressed uniform and flew to Boston. The first doctor was a pediatrician and he'd gone to Holy Cross. We really hit it off and went to lunch at the cafeteria. He spoke encouragingly. "You'll love it here," "We want maturity," and "We honor your service." Good lord, this is a piece of cake. Who's next? A neurologist. He sat behind a high desk as I sat on a low sofa looking up. Naturally. The furniture arrangement said, "I'm god, and I control your future." He skimmed my application and said, "Son, you have some set of balls. You blow up orphanages and hospitals and now want to soothe your conscience by becoming a doctor."

I had heard that during interviews some professors would try to rattle you with intimidation, and I instantaneously knew this was my gauntlet. It didn't take a second for me to revert to the Bronx and say, "Oh, Doctor, I only blew up a few, not a big deal, really." He must have known I was kidding and that I realized how insane his statement to me was. He couldn't be that stupid and vapid. I would learn over the years that this was the hallmark of many physicians.

He closed my folder and said, "That'll do. Good day." I didn't get into Harvard.

But I did get into Georgetown's School of Medicine. A true life-changer for me. But how could I pay for the tuition? I had one shot at having this happen. A visit to the CNO (Chief of Naval Operations). The big kahuna. His name was Admiral Elmo Zumwalt, and to me he was only two seats under god. I had to see him, but I surely didn't do it casually. My world-to-be rested in his hands. No guts no glory, so off I went with mega-sweaty armpits into the Pentagon and Admiral Zumwalt's palace.

A remarkably pleasant meeting with the admiral ended with him telling me that the Navy (he!) would pay for Georgetown and I would remain on active duty with all of those benefits. Holy sweet jeezuz! Are you snapping my shorts? How the hell could that be happening to me? But it was. I was off to Georgetown School of Medicine as a naval officer in the medical corps. Diane was ecstatic and immediately went about finding an apartment in Arlington, Virginia. By June of 1973 we were settled in Arlington and I was finishing up at Patuxent Test Center.

Medical school? I couldn't forget that I had never graduated from high school and graduated by the skin of my teeth with the lowest grade-point average ever from Holy Cross College. Now I was truly heading for the big leagues at Georgetown. Yes, the big leagues, but I was carrying a stick while needing a bat. Strike one!

Chapter Fourteen

The Big Leagues

"No patient cares how much you know until they know you care"

Medical school can be summed up with numerous descriptive words. They roll off the tongue of anyone who has endured it. Vomit, pain, tears, doubt, exhaustion, joy, failure, insecurity, and—so many more. There can be no explanation for that devastating gauntlet. Seriously lethal gauntlet. Medical students have an enormously high suicide rate. Depression is rampant. Divorce is as prevalent as the common cold. Add to that, the price of medical school can sum up to $400,000 for all four years. But the highest toll that I've noticed is the avarice and affluenza that take over for so many medical students. And the biggest loss can be empathy and kindness. It's as if many finish this four-year battle feeling entitled to an exorbitant salary, respect, and adulation. What happened to the humility we were taught for the gift we were given of caring for people at their most vulnerable? The M.D. doesn't stand for "Minor Deity." The gift of caring for the sick is not a blue-ribbon prize. It's meant to be an opportunity to give far more than one gets. The men and women who live that belief become amazing human beings and caregivers.

I bow to each and every one of them and am honored to have been treated by many of them.

But medical school is absolutely indescribable. The amount of memory needed is ridiculous. Your insecurity will never be higher, and it surges daily like a spreading plague. No relief and no comfort. Add to that your first human-to-human and human-to-cadaver interventions. The first time you pick up a scalpel and incise into a cadaver is a forever memory. More than one budding doctor has passed out or lost lunch at the first cut. Some, who have worked so hard to get there, must admit to themselves and proud relatives that this job is not for them. Social work, psychology, anything, but not this grotesque intimacy with another human being. Does the thought ever cross all medical students' minds that one day that would be them on the table? Absolutely. You must confront the fact that we all have feet of clay. Most of the world can go to work daily and suppress the thoughts of pain, illness, and death. Not a physician. He or she must face and be reminded of those realities every moment of the day. And if the medical student is married, as I was, the split-personality effect burrows in. Imagine a day filled with nonstop heavy academics, sleeplessness, anxiety, tests, and an intimate physical exam on a stranger. I still wasn't even sure of the name of the little thing hanging down in the back of your throat (uvula). But you have to fake it. After all, you're wearing a white jacket!

Walk into your apartment exhausted while your spouse tries to connect with you. The sink is leaking, and did you remember to fill out the insurance forms? Really? I can't even remember my own name. Or here's the whopper. I came home after one of those days only to be met by Diane with, "Guess what? I'm pregnant." After seven miscarriages, this was an amazing miracle. Even with that news, I only wanted to crash in bed. Later I would feel guilty about having to fake my excitement about the pregnancy, but exhaustion causes personality mutations in everyone. It's no excuse; it just flaunted my weakness. The faking must have worked because there were no repercussions and I slept the night.

Mark, my son, was born in January of 1974 and was the first-born in our medical class. He was immediately crowned the "Class of '77's mascot." The class all chipped in and filled my car with Pampers and formula. How silly. What kind of gift was that? Oh, I quickly learned what an amazing gift those pee-catchers were. What seemed like enough diapers to last through his high-school years Mark went through in a blink. Thank god for the Navy Exchange to replenish the diapers or I would have gone to Kleenex and duct tape. Pee, poop, and 2:00 a.m. feedings galore, I wouldn't trade a minute. Absolutely the best part and only part that I cherish about medical school.

Does medical school cloud your judgement? Try this one on for size. Shortly after Mark was delivered, he was taken to the nursery and I was allowed to view him through the glass window. In those days there was no such thing as spouses in the delivery suite. And as I gazed through the glass half crying and half overjoyed, my stupor was suddenly overtaken with panic. I noticed that the bottoms of Mark's feet were black. Not bruised, not brown: black. Holy crap, my son was infected with aspergillosis nigrans, a fungal infection. Damn, how in the hell had that happened? He would need antifungal meds and days of hospitalization. I flew to the door and called for the nurse in the hopes of getting immediate treatment for Mark.

"Sir, what are you talking about? What infection?" I calmly explained about the fungus on his feet and the need for an infectious disease consultation. She was such a sweetheart and must have dealt with hundreds of insane fathers, but probably not many medical students.

"Are you talking about the black ink-pad marks on your son's feet? We'll wipe that off shortly, but, of course, we footprint all newborns as soon as they're born."

Good god, could I have looked more ignorant? Footprint ink. Of course. But to me in my second semester of pathology, it was a clear case of fungal aspergillosis. My pulse dropped immediately; all was well with the world. It was a humbling and lasting reminder that for years to come I would learn more from seasoned nurses than I ever would from textbooks or arrogant physicians. I did think it best not to mention to my newborn son's nurse that I was a brilliant medical student. Some things are best kept to oneself.

Medical school came and went like a blink. Literally one blink to be precise, because that's about all the sleep any of us would get. In fact, the night before graduation, I had been up for 36 hours assisting at surgery and managing the chaos at D.C. General Indigent Hospital. I was a zombie. But now a zombie with M.D. after my name. I hoped I had learned that M.D. truly did not stand for "minor deity." And most importantly, I learned that the word "doctor" comes from the Latin meaning "teacher," not billing agent or prescriber.

And suddenly, after four years, I graduated. I was in 30 days of heaven. No "on call" sleepless nights, tests, oral exams, or duties. I had 30 days to play with Mark, who was now walking. I was actually writing "M.D." after my name without a single responsibility that goes with that title. The world could rest peacefully knowing that I, who knew almost nothing medically, could follow the Hippocratic maxim to "Do no harm."

Chapter Fifteen

Welcome Back To the Anchors Aweigh, Doc

"There are no secrets to success. It's the result of preparation, hard work, and learning from failure."
-Colin Powell

After 30 days of Nirvana, I was back in a Navy white uniform and Diane and I had moved into a small house in Bethesda, Maryland. Mark was in kindergarten and essentially so was I. I was a "newbie" intern, bottom-of-the-food-chain, scut-running, totally ignorant physician. Medicine and flying were similar in that regard. After years of flight training, you were awarded the coveted Navy wings of gold. Man, did you ever walk taller? With the ohs and ahs of many in the military seeing those wings, only you knew at that moment how inept an aviator you were. Yes, you could fly and navigate an aircraft and even land on an aircraft carrier. That all sounded good, but you were in fact a rookie and had not experienced anything other than CAVU (ceiling and visibility unlimited) perfect-situation flying. Not a bullet or missile had passed your aircraft's canopy. It would take time, experience and luck before you became a seasoned aviator. Well, guess what? An intern is in that same flight status.

As such, you were literally unsafe for patients. And here's the worst part: You knew it, too.

Medical school was brutal, but internship was inhumane. It's no wonder that alcoholism and divorce were rampant. Depending on the specialty, the level of inhumanity varies tremendously. Psychiatry? No sweat. Reasonable hours, home for dinner and able to sleep most nights on call in the hospital. Dermatology? Same.

Surgery, on the other hand, was an affliction and Calvary of its own. The hours and lack of sleep were a given, but I was in an unusual role as well. The newbie or intern in medicine was the "scut dog." His position made him the target for being constantly yelled at and berated. He would be given all the nasty jobs like opening and draining a rectal abscess. (Sorry if you're offended, but they happen and someone has to take care of them.) Simply put, you are the lowest of the low and can never do anything right. In a surgery case, the intern gets the glorified job of cutting the ends from the sutures that the staff physician has just tied. After cutting, invariably the surgeon yelled, "Too short!" or "Too long!" Once, in a fatigued state, the surgeon turned briskly to me and, holding the sutures up, yelled, "Cut, goddammit!" I quietly replied, "Yes, sir! Would you like them too short or too long?" He actually laughed, but said again, "Cut." Now truth be told, I would not have said that, but fatigue was cascading, and I had one big advantage over other interns. They were all straight out of medical school and young lieutenants new to the Navy. I was a senior lieutenant commander with aviator wings and ribbons on my uniform. "Who the hell is this guy anyway?" most were thinking. Especially the staff physicians wondered what I was doing there, and many were junior in grade. Once, a junior staff doctor semi-yelled at me. It sounded strange:

"Get those lab reports here for rounds today!—sir." "Sir" was always used as a sign of deference and respect when addressing a senior officer. And indeed I was his senior but also his lackey and scut dog. A very weird predicament, but at times I loved it and it paid off.

At 1500 (3:00 p.m.) one day in March 1978, I was paged to the Emergency Room. By now I was a seasoned surgical intern and expected anything. But not this! As soon as I arrived, the E.R. nurse led me to a curtained gurney. Pulling back the gurney, I saw a young woman crying, rolling in pain. Gallbladder? Appendectomy? Nope. It was my wife, Diane, in labor. She was an absolutely lovely woman, but she handled pregnancy like most would handle the Black Plague. No put-down here; I'm sure the pain was amazing, but the screaming was overwhelming. A quick exam by the OB resident and staff doctor and she was on her way to delivery. Unfortunately, the labor was prolonged and the exclamations from her pain would have made a priest cringe. To the O.R. for a C-section. But on the way, she somewhat fainted and, whammo, our daughter was here. Kristy Ann Schneider was the latest U.S. Navy recruit at Bethesda Naval Hospital. What a love. Mark took to his little sister rather like a young boy getting his first puppy dog. He was always checking on her and asking to do things for her. There was only a four-year difference between the two, but what a difference that timespan made. Yes, as the years fell by, they certainly had their spats. I remember that one time Mark put tabasco sauce in Kristy's milkshake, and if Kristy had had a gun, Mark would be carrying lead. But move forward 40 years and you'll find the kindest brother and sister team on the planet. Want to know if you win as a parent? If your children end up loving each other and watching out for one another, place your gold cup on the mantel. You win big time.

By the end of surgical internship, I was too pooped to pop. As much as I loved surgery and my patients, I was spent. And truthfully, for as little time as I spent with Mark and Kristy during internship, Diane had to carry the load. And it was taking its toll.

I was offered the surgical residency, which was prestigious. My goal at that point was to specialize in either pediatric surgery or cardiothoracic surgery. Unfortunately, the Navy had other plans. They needed general surgeons and no pediatric or cardiothoracic doctors. I understood the rationale because the mission of the military is for combat casualties. I was headed for general surgery.

That reality coupled with total exhaustion and stress had me doubting my choice of a career in medicine. Delta Airlines was looking pretty damned good right then. And then, as in most of my life, something happened and suddenly I was able to stand again. This time it was Doug and Louise. Doug was a Vietnam vet who showed up in the E.R. of Bethesda Naval Hospital one late evening. It was that time of day when my body was a dust rag and my brain flipped between anger and stupor. Any interruption in your survival mode at that hour engendered gut-raw irritation. Doug was mine. Called to the E.R., I was trigger-pulled to pissed. I'm done, I told myself. I will not accept the General Surgery residency regardless of the prestige. That quickly, my decision was made. I had no clue what I would do but I was through with this non-life.

I saw Doug in an E.R. cubicle that I was well familiar with as this year was ending. I had been there every other night on call for the past year and then spent most of the sleepless nights assisting in the operating room. That night would be no different. Doug was a mess. Overweight, unshaven, disheveled, and drunk. He had garbled speech and a foul smell. Most of my attempts to gather information from him were met with f--- and s--- cursing to leave him alone. Perfect. We agree on something! But my job was not to cure or criticize: It was to care. This would be a tough one.

I noticed his feet were filthy, but beneath the dirt his toes and heels looked blue. Of course there were many other signs, but with a temperature of 103 and blood sugar through the roof, even a young rookie doctor such as I knew this was a catastrophic emergency. I called to prepare the operating room and for the chief resident and staff doctor. By the time they arrived, the labs were back and confirmed the diagnosis of sepsis. Sepsis is bacteria in the blood invading one's organs. Mortality is generally 85 percent. Doug was in a short race with death. He had no family and only a neighbor had found him and brought him to the E.R.

By 3:00 a.m. I was sitting at his bedside. We had amputated both feet and started two antibiotics intravenously. I remember looking at his bruised arms and his old tattoos and wondering what was written on the pages of this veteran's life. He remained pretty sedated with only an eye opening, occasionally, as I stroked his arm. Was he crying? Why? I would never know. I sat there stroking his arm, imagining his life, and I became sadder and sadder. And really furious. Where the hell was his family as he lay here dying? Me. Only me. So I started to cry. It was a crying that I didn't want to stop. Then I felt a hand on my shoulder. It was Louise, the senior floor nurse. She leaned forward and whispered words I'll never forget: "You did all you could, Doctor. You are going to be fine. I'd be happy to have you as my doctor." God, could there ever be kinder words? That's all it took. The kindest words to me from the kindest woman and Louise had breathed life into me. I now had an idea of where I belonged.

Doug died that morning. More would die in the years to come. At such a meaningful moment in a patient's life, their dying, I knew that I was intimately a member of their family. What a unique honor.

The gauntlet year taught me the need to look at and see the whole patient, who was not her gallbladder or his appendix. I would pursue Family Medicine. It happened that the Family Medicine residency was at the Naval Hospital in Charleston, South Carolina. They had already accepted their candidates, but one was recently diagnosed with lymphoma and could not attend. Tragic, but he would recover and enter again in two years. Enter Tom. I was on my way to Charleston with Diane, Mark, and Kristy.

A second internship was devastating, but as an intern in Family Medicine, I was on overnight call every third or fourth night. Compared to my year in surgery, this was like being awarded a year's holiday in Hawaii. The biggest factor, of course, was the sanity factor. I had one year under my belt, so there was not much that would shake me. And I quickly enjoyed having clinic patients that I could follow to watch their progress. Surgery was more of a slam-bam, cut-and-go, bring on the next patient. In those days, in family practice, I delivered my own pregnant patients and then took care of the infant. It was amazingly satisfying. The other wonderful factor was the demeanor and kindness of my fellow intern/residents and supervising staff. There was virtually no place for put-downs or snide remarks. We were all there to help each other, learn together and care for every patient. It was a remarkable environment for learning and caring for patients.

But what's that old maxim: "All good things must come to an end"? After graduation from the Family Medicine residency three years later, I was quite senior in rank as a commander, but a relative fledgling in medicine. What would the Navy in its infinite wisdom do with me? The answer was Newport, Rhode Island. The Navy War College was there as well as Officer Candidate School. A beautiful spot to live, but the assignment was to start a Family Medicine clinic there. Great. A new clinic to handle a slew of military families. I was to be given one nurse, one enlisted corpsman, and how many doctors? Me! One physician recently out of his residency and at best a medical novice with no experience running a clinic.

By this time, in 1981, perhaps five staff members in the Newport Naval Hospital had heard of "family practice" and none knew what we did. The learning process was arduously slow. Our clinic was up and rolling, and patients loved it. They loved it to the point that we had to decline to take new patients. Word traveled fast that there was one doctor that could take care of Mom, Dad, and children. But when the hospital staff found out what a family-practice physician could do, we became the "go to" for coverage. If the pediatrician was taking leave (vacation), our clinic suddenly became a pediatric overflow clinic. The same was true for all of the hospital specialties. There was no respite, and my staff handled it all like heroes. Truly remarkable people.

Newport was fantastic for my family. Compared to residencies, I had much more time for Mark and Kristy. It seemed like the kind of family time I had hoped for. Picnics were a regular routine on weekends, and I could occasionally sneak in a sail on the gorgeous rough waters around Newport. This change in milieu was a time for reflection. What's next? Is it time to leave the Navy? Where are the answers?

It was time to do some snooping. I called my detailer (an officer who sends orders for your next duty). My detailer, very forthright, told me that as a senior commander I would probably be assigned to an aircraft carrier or the Pentagon. No more patient-care medicine. Time for administrative duties.

Total yuck, in my books. But timing and luck have such an amazing effect on our lives, and particularly mine. I had traveled to D.C. for a conference and I was giving a talk to Navy docs. After my time on stage, one of the Head and Neck Otolaryngology staff physicians came up to me to express how much he enjoyed the humor in my talk. He always fell asleep in these conferences but loved staying awake and laughing. I thanked him profusely and recognized him. His name tag read "Dr. Robert Lee." He reminded me that as a surgical resident years before I had assisted him on a difficult thyroid surgery. I had no clue, but nodded politely. "Why didn't you go into 'head and neck,' Tom?" he asked. I have no idea how my words came out or where the bull came from, but I said, "Dr. Lee, I was waiting for you to become the Department Chief." I smiled but he didn't. After a pause, he said, "Tom, I am the Chief and it's not too late. One of our residents dropped out and we need to fill the spot. The residency starts in two weeks. Can I convince you to take the spot?" Word for word, that's how it happened.

Back in Newport I asked Diane if she could take a joke. "Tom, what are you talking about?" "Diane, we have two weeks to move to D.C. I'm starting another residency in head and neck surgery. I'm not sure entirely what those surgeons do, but it'll keep me off the rolling seas." She took the joke and off we went to D.C.

Ten days later I was driving through New York with Mark and Kristy and one parakeet heading to Bethesda, Maryland. Diane was driving our old station wagon, filled to the brim with whatever didn't fit in the moving vans. Diane was miles ahead when Mark asked me a challenging question. He asked, "Dad, was there really a Billy Ruzza?" Billy was, of course, my favorite grammar-school friend, but I hadn't seen him in 35 years. Billy and I, as mentioned, were always getting into trouble. But I used those faux pas to impress my children about principles such as honesty or truth. The stories were endless, and so Mark's skepticism was not surprising. Unfortunately for Mark, his father loved an intellectual challenge. There was no GPS in those days. There were phone books at gas stations that were more like the encyclopedia. But after a tad of searching, I found Billy's address, and he was 15 minutes away. Off we went to see my best grammar-school friend. The rest of the story has been told but it was a moment that my children and I will never forget. Neither would Billy!

Finally settled in Bethesda, I was now a senior-ranking first-year resident in head and neck surgery. And for the first year, on call was every two to three nights with little sleep but lots of Dr. Peppers and cheddar-cheese-combo pretzels. Weight gain galore! By the second year, on call went to every fourth night. A chance to breathe. I loved surgery and being in the operating room, but family practice had spoiled me practicing as a surgeon. Seeing an illness such as laryngeal cancer couldn't wash the principles of family practice out of my head. I was plagued with wanting to know who this patient was. Married? His fear level hearing of his cancer? How can I keep him from smoking? I needed to speak to his family. Most of all, I was plagued with the question of how to prevent this disease. Surgery was fine, but it was only a Band-Aid. Patients should never get the disease in the first place. It reminded me of flying in Vietnam and hearing about one of my buddies getting shot down. All of us rationalized his death by saying things like, "He really wasn't that good of a pilot. I would have evaded that missile." And yet we knew better. It was self-chat that let us get up and fly again tomorrow. Truth be told, that pilot should have prevented that shoot-down. But how? By never flying in a war in the first place. Now I know that will never happen, but it's true. Just as I know the likelihood of the cancer patient giving up smoking was slim at best. Preventive health care before the disaster happens is a hard sell. We all want to seek pleasure and avoid pain, and, I can attest, smoking, alcohol, and overeating along with many other "Sirens of Homer" are Achilles' heels. Those "pleasures" were fulfilling a need. Simply removing them would only leave another void. We need to fill that void with a drive. For me, it was rowing crew, exercise, triathlons, reading, traveling with my family and—friends. Companionship. The point is that you must fill the void.

The entire four years of the Head and Neck Surgery residency was another gauntlet. No sleep, lots of Cokes, Combos, and way too little sleep. All the stress, diet, and lack of sleep, plus my career as an aviator in a war, would take its toll, and heavily, within a few short years. But let's not spoil that party quite yet.

Graduation from the residency meant new orders. Normally, like the other residents, I would be assigned to an aircraft carrier or major teaching hospital. Always dependent on the needs of the Navy. My choice was San Diego, California. My orders weren't for there, though. Because of my seniority and aviation background, I was being sent to the home of naval aviation: Pensacola, Florida. Yes, I could do surgery and practice Otolaryngology Head and Neck Surgery, but my seniority now required me to administrate.

Administrate the hospital? Why not send me to do engine maintenance on the new F-18 fighter jet? I was competent in neither field. Pick up and move, new schools for the kids, new friends and a tad more stress. Not many civilians realize how difficult a military life is on a family. Only around 2 percent of this country's population has ever served in the military, and most Americans are now openly proud and thankful for our military. It's a wonderful thing to see. Coming back from Vietnam was a horrific experience particularly because of the disdain returning vets were shown. But whatever era a vet is, or has served, she and her entire family have paid a price that few will understand. I salute each and every one.

My tour in Pensacola was a bit of a quagmire for me. On the one hand, I was able to be a surgeon, with all of its benefits. And the senior physician of the entire hospital. You were feared as the head of the hospital and as a Navy captain. And so if you happened to be kind and just with the staff, you were loved as a saint. Unfortunately, too many who attain that position become megalomaniacs. Power and prestige are vicious enticements for cruelty and arrogance. Such was the demeanor of the officer I was replacing. As long as I didn't spit on the floors, the staff would support and respect me because of the behavior of their prior commanding officer.

Knowing nothing about administration, the best strategy was honesty. I gathered the administrative staff and confessed my complete dependence on them to help us make Pensacola the flagship hospital in the Navy. All hands on deck, and they jumped at the opportunity. We had a myriad of administrative and medical successes due entirely to our incredible self-sacrificing hospital staff. A weird issue today perhaps, but in 1988 changing the hospital to an "all non-smoking facility" was fraught with debate. Nonetheless, the staff voted for that monumental change. As the commanding officer, I could have merely ordered it so. But how remarkable to have it be a staff decision. The staff felt so empowered. The Navy issues orders, not votes.

The other fantastic aspect of my tour was that I could perform as a physician and surgeon. Taking off the uniform, I could don surgery scrubs and become one of the staff. This was another opportunity to make inroads. It's unfortunate, but many surgeons feel entitled to the arrogance and haughty disposition that seems to drape surgeons. If I've heard it once, I've heard it repeatedly from nurses and staff: "Doctor Smith is so mean and cruel I hate working with him! But he is such a good surgeon." No! He is not a good surgeon. Good surgeons are kind and appreciate their staff. The others are flat-out jerks and I don't want them cutting on me.

Regardless of the scrubs, the entire operating room staff knew who I was. It was easy to see the tiptoeing around and special treatment that the staff tried to provide. "Captain, I'm so sorry that your operating room is running later with an earlier surgery. We're calling in more staff to open another room for you, sir." My reply was something like, "Not at all, Nancy. Please don't call anyone in. I really enjoy just being here and I have a ton of reading to catch up on. I'll let the patient know we're running a bit behind. But thank you so much." "Captain, I can tell the patient for you." "Oh, I'm happy to chat with my patient. You have tons to do. I don't want him to think I'm reading up on how to do the procedure." The point was that I did not want special treatment and appreciated everything that they did. A very simple truthful axiom of kindness grew and spread to where we all became part of a thoughtful family. And being part of the medical staff gave great credibility. When I had to make tough calls that would affect the staff, such as canceling vacations, I wasn't only a pain-in-the-butt administrator who didn't understand what that meant to them. I was one of them and my vacation was canceled as well.

It was during those days in 1988 that I began short traveling stints to other hospitals, giving talks on a variety of topics. My staff had made Pensacola Hospital an eyecatcher for other hospitals in the country. The traveling was a double-edged sword, though. Unfortunately, if you're a physician and you give humorous talks rather than mundane fact-filled academics, women have a tendency to want to become a "groupie." It doesn't matter how you look or how much money you have; they often want to be connected. I'm not proud to admit it, but I fell prey to the candy. My own home relationship had gone down the road of completely platonic. No fighting or meanness, just—nothing. One of the truly sad times in my life happened during these years. I had met Alycia. She was 15 years younger than I and classically stunning, extremely intelligent, and quick on her toes. Kindness was her middle name. We had spoken about marriage, but truthfully, as the years rolled quickly by, I began doubting how long I would survive some of the medical calamities that befell me. But the bliss was amazing. And yet it was not to last. I hadn't heard from her in a few weeks. Although I knew she was busy with her career, we usually talked on the phone every two or three days. No calls. Finally I called her brother. The news destroyed me. She had died in a corporate plane crash in Colorado three weeks before. I had missed the funeral and there was no one for me to ache with. But ache I did, for months turning to years.

Without a doubt, commanding the Naval Hospital was a joy beyond joys. The entire environment of the hospital reeked with kindness and benevolence. Yes, there were many abrasive moments, but such is the way with people. Did I mention that people are crazy? For example, I received a 2:00 a.m. call from the Pensacola police. "Sir, do you have a Dr. Blank on your staff at the hospital?" I certainly did. He was the chief of our anesthesia department, a top-notch doctor although a tad squirrely. It seems he had been arrested at the local Walmart for stealing ten pairs of running shorts. He had put them all on in the dressing room and tried to walk out unnoticed. Good grief, Charlie Brown! And here's the kicker: He had the police call me because he had no friends or family to vouch for him. Now this was a board-certified anesthesiologist who was earning a damned good salary. He was up for promotion to commander. He certainly wasn't earning a civilian doctor's salary, but he didn't need a dime more to live well. Why steal running shorts? Our psychiatrist claimed that it was his way of calling for help. Those who steal are looking for love and attention. Well, Dr. Blank certainly got the attention. A civil charge and lawyer fees were bad enough, but it would go into his military record. No promotion, and a recommendation for an administrative discharge without benefits from the Navy for "conduct unbecoming an officer." I hated writing for his dismissal, but his actions had set that course. There was an appeal. A good man, a great physician, but a gentleman who needed therapy far more than he needed a naval career.

Aside from the potholes of the job, I was traveling and commanding a great hospital in a lovely part of the country. Seriously, what could go wrong? What an absurd statement for me to make regarding my life. But it seems as though mine is a domino life, as, I suppose, is everyone's. One event cascading into another, like it or not.

I was in the home of naval aviation, and although not flying anymore, jet fuel was still in my veins. I watched the students taking off and landing at the airfield that was close to the hospital. And every Tuesday and Wednesday, the Blue Angels had a practice show over the base. The "boss" (commanding officer) of the Blues was an aviator I knew from my flight days. Gil Rud was truly a remarkably skilled pilot and, more importantly, one hell of a great gentleman.

I was called to the E.R. one afternoon because Gil had sliced his right index finger. A complete home accident that all of us have probably done at some time. This time, though, it was on the flight hand of the Blue Angels' boss and not a simple cut but a tendon laceration. I had a staff of four very qualified orthopedists, but Dr. Tom Westphal was the youngest and clearly the most adept. Surgeons either have it or they don't. They can operate using a soup-can lid and shoestring with perfect results. Other docs are generally adequate, but not gifted. Tom was gifted. A quick call to Tom and we were in the O.R. immediately. He did an exquisite repair and it was fun having an old friend like Gil babbling nonsense under "twilight" anesthesia. A problem: How would Gil recover without moving his right hand and still lead the team?

Tom curved a splint for Gil's hand around a flight stick from an F-18 fighter jet. Then we had the aviation crew reconfigure the tension on the control stick. In four days, Tom gave Gil the thumbs up, or index finger up, I guess, and Gil flew a successful practice with the team. Of course, there was no publicity because in those days, what happened to the Blues stayed with the Blues. But true to his style, Gil came over weeks later and offered Tom a demonstration flight with the Blues, and my guess is that Tom is still foaming at the mouth. Success is a wonderful thing, even when there's no marching band to celebrate.

Shortly after that, in 1989, Gil called me to his office in the Blues' hangar. I remember the glorious smell of aviation fuel and paint as I walked up the ladder to his office. It seemed that his flight doctor who took care of the team was having difficulties. It's a brutal job with all the traveling and always being in the spotlight. You were also having to treat some who felt they were prima donnas. A flight doc's nickname throughout the Navy was "the quack." A term of endearment, I think. But not always. The task and joy of a naval aviator is flying, but the flight quack could ground a pilot at any time for almost anything. Thus they became the police of the air.

So what to do with a front-page member of the Blues who was breaking down? I told Gil that we could put him in our hospital clinic and watch him and all of the patients he was seeing. That pleased the "boss" and it would all be kept hush-hush. But what about the team and the flight support crew? Who could take care of them for any sicknesses? Good question, Gil. "You'd need a doc who understands flight medicine, is board-certified in Family Medicine, and, most importantly, can keep his mouth shut." Gil was sharp and quickly replied, "Okay, Doc, what's it gonna cost me?" Ahh, my chance to slam the hammer. "Well, I was thinking a few flights in air shows would pretty much cover the tab, Boss." Done deal. And what a great chance to smell and inhale JP-4 jet fumes into my lungs again. More fun than can be described.

But all of the fun and flights with the Blues brought my memory up to date about my flying history. As much as I loved the team and the flying, even as a load (passenger), I was always wary. My flight ogres would never leave me and as it turns out, rightly so.

The highlight of the Blues' year is the end-of-the-year air show and party over the Pensacola base. It had been a great year and the festivities were set. I had been given the honor of flying in the "7" jet (usually it had been the "4" jet). The F-18 is a single-seat jet, but the "7" is two-seated for training and "guest loads." Don C. would be the pilot in command, and we would be flying in the "slot" position, right behind the boss who led in jet number 1.

Gorgeous day, my family had VIP seating, and the team was electric. The first half of the show was flawless, and then the Tom ogre showed up. We were doing a maneuver called the "left echelon transition role." A different language that means all four jets were aligned staggering back from the Boss. This echelon formation then climbs over the crowd and transitions, while upside down, back to the four-plane diamond formation.

While inverted, we started to transition and Don C. hit the wing of the "3" jet. Our canopy immediately shattered and we fell out of the formation and came screaming toward the ground. I grabbed the "B ring" (a black and yellow cord over your head that, when pulled, will eject you from the aircraft). I hit the mic and told Donny I was set to eject. He deftly rolled the aircraft upright and we avoided the ground. We pulled off to the quiet side runway where a backup jet was ready to go. We finished the show, but in the debrief, well, no need to go into details, but it wasn't a happy review. The only fun from that major boo-boo came at the after-season party. Dr. Tom W. and I were invited and took the opportunity to roast the team. When it came to me touching on the mid-air collision, I looked at Donny from the stage and told him how sorry I was for messing things up. I said, "Donny, I could have sworn that I heard the Boss call for us to break off from the formation and join up on

'Fat Albert.'" Fat Albert was the C-130 supply aircraft that followed the Blues everywhere with parts and gear. Of course there would never be a join-up on Fat Albert, but it grabbed a laugh about a horrific mistake during an air show. Definitely life-threatening.

I certainly didn't need another reminder that aviation was probably not in my best interest, but that one clearly stung and left me with a few sleepless nights. On the other hand, my son and daughter thought it was "cool." Youth is a wonderful thing.

It was shortly after the mid-air collision in 1989 that I was sitting at my desk and "God was in his heaven, all was right with the world." I had made the mental decision that Pensacola would be my last command, even if I were to be selected for admiral. My children were in the midst of high school and another move would be above and beyond the call of duty for them. They were first in my life and always have been. With that as background, the letter sitting on my desk became more of a hand grenade. It was from the Surgeon General in D.C. I wanted to put it aside to attend a barbecue I was having for the hospital staff on the quadrangle near the E.R. But let's be real. You don't postpone opening a letter from the Surgeon General. A quick tear-open and a speed read, followed by two slower reads. The Surgeon General was ordering me to leave my position and move to D.C. as his adjutant. The implication, of course, was if I played my cards well I would be the next Surgeon General.

It's worth taking a moment to scrutinize this "gift." The Surgeon General was in trouble. He was the leader of the Navy's medical staff, the head honcho. Senior to him was the Secretary of the Navy, followed by the Vice-President and President. These were the power players. But the Navy and Marine Corps made up the "line" staff: the Aviators, Ship's Company, Ground Pounders, Tankers, and so on. These are the true gunpowder of our military force. And this "force" was thoroughly pissed. No other way to put it. The admirals and generals were not getting first-class medical care for their troops. The newbie doctors being sent to care for the troops had little or no military training. No saluting or marching style, no "Yes sir, no sir" respect. In short, the doctors were fulfilling an obligation and biting at the bit to get out and go into private practice. There were very few in my boat with a line corps background and a love for treating military personnel. The Surgeon General needed a physician with combat experience and line corps lineage to deal with the generals and admirals. Someone they would listen to. It helped that I had written a paper on exactly this conflict three years earlier. The paper recommended mandatory deployment of specialists for our troops. Enhance Officer Candidate School for Physicians, Dentists, and Lawyers. It went over like a lead fart at the time, but now the line was demanding it.

Where did that leave me? The soup ingredients in this bowl came down to, first, I could not move my children again. Becoming Admiral would mean three more years of active service. I still had one-and-a-half years left on my current orders, and we were making huge strides at turning Naval Hospital Pensacola into a "flagship."

No, it wasn't an easy decision. My ego was pointing a sword in my back. Admiral Schneider! It had a nice ring to it. So, yes, I struggled. But discussing this with my children made it an automatic response for me. Diane was opposed to the move as well, but we were going through the initial moves of separation and divorce. It would be a few years before it happened, but the seeds were already sprouting, and admittedly, I was the fertilizer.

So my simple reply letter to the Surgeon General was filled with gratuities and deference, but it clearly said "No, thank you." Easy-peasy, right? Surely his reply would send me "best wishes." Nope. Not even close. The Surgeon General replied with a vitriolic demand. The phrases sounded a lot like, "What didn't you understand, Captain?," "This is an honor," "This is not a request," "Consider this a direct order"! Uh-oh, this wasn't going to be pretty. Perhaps a respectful phone call would put this to rest. (Yes, I was still naïve.)

My call to the S.G. was sickening. It left me nauseated. I knew after the call that this man was not one I wanted to work for. I was being chosen to make him look good and to hell with my needs. I explained about my children and 26 years of prior naval service and moving. "I don't give a goddamn about your kids. They're not going to be my adjutant. Leave there."

Many will criticize my next moves, and I can't justify them, but the S.G. said the magic words of my final straw. He told me he'd make the decision easy for me. Either I show up in ten days or I'd be sent to an aircraft carrier for the 18 months left on my contract. Needless to say, I was pissed. Pissed? No, I was looking for a Phantom with missiles to use against this blackmailing S.G. But he was my superior and I was subject to his orders. Or was I?

Years before when stationed at Bethesda Naval Hospital, I was called to the E.R. to see a young man with a perforated eardrum. I repaired the eardrum and became friends with the young man, J.B. As with the rest of my life, serendipity came around for a cold beer. J.B. had climbed the political ladder and was now the Secretary of the Navy. Dare I break the chain of command and present my case to him? There could be only two outcomes. I would be retired from the Navy with 26 years of active duty, or I would be charged with breaking the chain of command and be sent to Leavenworth prison.

Vietnam left many with internal scars and none of them gave one peace, particularly not for me. It did leave me with an anger always boiling and right at the edge of my anger pot, like soup that's beyond ready. You must keep your eye on it constantly, or, well, you know that mess. And so it was with the S.G. Had he simply phoned politely and asked for my help in his dreadful position, not to garner more rank stripes but because our troops needed the best, I would have been at his service. The troops were putting it on the line every day and second-rate care was criminal. "Yes, sir," I would have replied. "I'll explain to my family and somehow we'll make it work." But that's not what was said. No. He blackmailed me with 18 more months at sea duty on a carrier. And as the commanding officer of the Naval Hospital, I would have to legally sign out of my orders and leave the hospital without a commanding officer. There wouldn't be a replacement for at least eight months. Commanding officers can't just be picked from a tree, though I've met some who, I swear, hung from a walnut tree.

The smart move would have been to phone the S.G. and explain that we got off on the wrong foot. My bad. Let's try again. But that would be the smart move, not the Tom move. I was down-and-dirty furious. "Pissed," by the way, is how you feel when you fall down while skiing on a blue slope. Furious for me is when I sense or smell injustice or arrogance. I was furious. Time for weapons "hot."

I took a sleepless night deciding on my next course, and by the next day I had my Rolodex in hand, and the Secretary of the Navy, J.B., was on the top of the spin. I made the call, and J.B.'s adjutant scheduled a lunch in two days. Tickets bought, uniform impeccably squared away, followed by excessive diarrhea. This was seriously petrifying for me and my family. I had no clue how this would end.

The following Friday found me walking the halls of the Pentagon in my dress blue uniform. It stood in stark contrast to my sheet-white face and dripping hands. This was a do-or-die scenario with my life and my family's in the balance. I was ushered into the Secretary's suite by a Marine colonel who was holding a Dictaphone and yellow pad and pen. I'm not sure why he needed all the paraphernalia. Worried that the battery in the recorder would fail?

Seriously, I can recall only tidbits of my lunch with J.B. I know I didn't eat a bite. J.B. remembered when I had cared for him at Bethesda when he was a young officer. I had lost all touch with him after he resigned his commission and left for the political sector as a civilian. He was kindly appreciative of my care for him and I remember trying to add some levity by replying that "Sometimes I get lucky." It worked.

My summary to J.B. was simple. I would accept his decision gratefully. I was there because of my perception of injustice. I was there because of my rank and, frankly, my connection. But what happens to my sailors? A pregnant wife, and her sailor is launched to Guam without her. His rank doesn't allow an accompanying wife. He has no choice but to go to Guam. Now I get it. Needs of the naval service come first, and orders are orders. Words every military person has heard from the moment they raise their hand and swear in. But where are the brains and heart of the military? Where are the spaces for exceptions? Where are the listeners for the unheard? Yes, I was still torqued. I left J.B. believing he cared and that intimidation was no way to run a navy. Win, lose, or draw, I had my time and I would peacefully accept my fate. The flight back to Pensacola was in a coma state, but the next three days were excruciating. Leavenworth? Oh well, at least I had some friends there serving time for military blunders. That thought kept me up every night.

On Day Three following my visit with the Secretary of the Navy, at 10:00 a.m. I was summoned out of my staff meeting to accept and sign for a certified letter from the Department of Defense. J.B.'s decision.

I opened the letter in the privacy of the captain's suite and read with delight that prison was not my fate. Nor was an aircraft carrier to be my path. The Secretary of the Navy mandated that I be retired with full honors and benefits within the next few weeks. Holy cow! What an amazing change. The command would be put in the hands of a great administrator and I would be a civilian. Something I had not experienced in 26 years. Diane and the kids were elated and I was numb. Okay, what now? Mark and Kristy wanted to stay in Pensacola and finish school. Diane was very happy with that plan because she had made many good friends there. (Personally, I was hoping for New England, Annapolis, or Williamsburg, Virginia.) It's hard to explain the transition from 26 years of a military career to suddenly diving into the civilian medical community. I learned the hard way that there was a distinct difference between the two communities. My retirement ceremony was laden with tradition and emotions. There was a ceremonial dinner that was a "roast" of me that went on late into the night. A formal inspection of the entire staff took place in front of the hospital and the Blue Angels just "happened" to do a fly-by during the ceremony. Yes, I openly teared up as I was "piped" ashore by my staff. I marched through the piping to meet Mark, Kristy, and Diane. A new life. The civilian path would be a stark contrast to my previous life.

As an aside, I mentioned friends in Leavenworth. Unfortunately, the hard politics of the military can be incredibly harsh. An example was the incident of my locker mate in the surgeons' changing room at Bethesda. His name was Don Billig, and he was new to the Navy. He was a certified cardiac surgeon and the teaching chairman of the cardiac surgery residency program. He was extremely well trained in the civilian sector and decided he wanted to serve his country. We had a great relationship in the locker room, and although hard-nosed in the operating room, he had a great sense of humor with me. Unfortunately, he had no patience for incompetence or inefficiency, and he made it clear to all around him. If an untrained nurse was assigned to his case that day, he had no qualms about yelling and throwing her out of the operating room. When asked to complete administrative duties, he would flatly refuse and rip the administrator a new orifice for suggesting it. This went on and on, but he was difficult to discipline while he was a commander and chair of the cardiac surgery program. He was renowned for taking on the most difficult cases rather than let a patient dwindle to death. As a consequence, some of his patients had terminal outcomes. The final straw came when a senior captain administrator came to his office and slammed a pile of papers on his desk and demanded that he complete them before leaving that night. Don took the stack, threw the papers in his face, and said, "Get the fuck out of my office and take this shit with you. And when you can open a man's heart and repair it, then I'll do your job, your goddamn paperwork."

The administration had had enough and decided to press charges against him through a legal court-martial. The facts were obscured and the charges were absurd, such as treason. Bottom line,

Billig was convicted and sent immediately to Leavenworth Penitentiary for ten years at hard labor. Holy god! I couldn't believe it. But off he went. I was back in my really-pissed-off mood but knew well enough the politics surrounding his case. So I was determined to stay in touch. I routinely wrote to him, and, of course, my letters were all pre-read before he received them. I sent him Gary Larson cartoon calendars telling him I thought a calendar was exactly what he needed. He sent me back a drawing of a fist with the middle finger raised and hahahaha. I also sent him an "Uncle Milton's" ant farm. I particularly liked that one and even bought one for my children. Amazing little critters. I couldn't help thinking that Don would release them into the prison. I also sent him a small index-card file with a note saying that I heard prisoners could use a "file" and I hoped that this would work. I know, it was a cheesy joke, but anything helps in prison.

I went to all three of Don's parole board hearings and the first two were flatly denied. Then he hired a hotshot civilian lawyer and, voila, he was not only released and exonerated, but given his rank back and back pay. He was free at last and he and his girlfriend left for Jamaica. And here's the kicker: I've never heard another word from Donny boy. What a time, what a tragedy, what a tale of travesty: His charges were all overturned.

But I digress.

I was officially retired from the Navy and looking for a local job in Pensacola so the kids could stay for high school. How hard could that be? Not to blow my own horn, but I was board-certified in Family Medicine, Otolaryngology Head and Neck Surgery, Preventive Medicine, and was in fellowships for Obesity Medicine and Pain Management. Okay, maybe I couldn't qualify for

McDonald's head chef, but I could sure as hell put a Band-Aid on patients. But evidently not in Pensacola. Pensacola is a small southern burg that is amazingly provincial. It took a while, but I've grown to really like the town and the good friends who live there. The mindset, however, as anywhere, can be stifling. Probably true in most small towns without much diversity. So here comes Tom with a Navy career behind him and multiple academic residencies. I was naïvely hoping for a standing ovation and ended up with a bucket of ice water to the face. No one and no medical group wanted to touch me. "There's not enough business here, Tom. We don't need any more doctors." Really? I had promised my children we'd stay. Hidden from them were the offers I had received from all over New England. So what to do? Take out a loan and set up a small office in Milton, Florida, outside Pensacola. At that time it was an extremely indigent area. Poverty and homelessness were rampant. But in no time I was a one-man doc in the boondocks. I loved the patients and remember many stories that touch the heart. I recall a mother who came to me with her deaf three-year-old daughter. Her daughter had longstanding thick fluid behind her eardrums because her mom couldn't afford doctor visits. The word was out, though, that I would see patients without money. This mom was so proud that when she heard I would have to operate on her daughter's ears she offered to sell her jalopy to pay. I told her she was lucky because that day was "free for single moms day" and she made it just in time. Keep the jalopy.

I was fully steeped in private practice and all of its horrors. Insurance, malpractice, equipment, staff, and a ton more. But the biggest change for me was the loss of camaraderie. Civilian doctors were all competing with each other and the mantra was "everyone for themselves" regardless of the cost. A searing example for me occurred when a patient of mine came to me tearfully explaining that she had been seen in the E.R. and the doctor who saw her said to come back to see him in three days. She asked if she could come see me instead and he replied, "I don't recommend it because Dr. Schneider isn't certified and he has AIDS." I convinced her that none of that was true, but my rage was at geyser level. I went to the E.R. and confirmed what happened with one of the E.R. nurses. She was embarrassed and told me she hadn't believed it but she didn't know what to do. No problem. I'd handle it. I know this sounds crazy, but I still had unbridled anger looking for a racetrack. He would serve the purpose.

I went to Dr. P.'s office late one afternoon in September 1990 to confront him. I was asked to take a seat in the waiting room, a request I completely disregarded. I walked into his back office and stood in front of his leather desk. After a few minutes he came in and sat down babbling niceties in a soupy southern drawl. I explained the purpose of my visit and he immediately denied it, with the usual nervous responses of "Tom, she's crazy. I would never do that. Nothing but lies." I let him finish and then showed the evidence of statements from the E.R. nurse and the patient. He turned white and continued to deny. I then took a different tack. I agreed with him. I made comments like, "Only an insecure slimeball would have said that, so the witnesses must be wrong." And here's where it gets crazy. I reached under my white physicians' coat and pulled out my military .45 revolver and pointed it at his forehead. (Yes, I had taken the shell clip out of the gun.) I then said to him that in case there was a speck of truth in my patient's and the nurse's comments, I needed him to know that this is how I handled conflicts such as this. One defaming word, one call to the police, one other slur, and I would "blow your f---ing head off. No threat, just a sick veteran's promise." Understood? A very panicked nod from a white ghost face is what I saw.

Crazy? For sure, but I never heard another peep from him in the next 20 years. Only a friendly smile and wave in the occasional passing. Years later, I am sorry for what I did. No, that's a lie. I don't regret a word.

Private practice: What a joy! But in 35 years of surgery and clinical practice, I was never sued. Why? My incredible skill? No, sir. I learned early on that patients don't care what you know until they know that you care. It's that simple, but impossible to teach to young doctors. Medicine is a caring calling, not a job.

At the risk of sounding ridiculous, it's important to know how ruthless private civilian practice can become. My own private practice in Pensacola took off. I was overwhelmed. None of the other practices would cover night call for me so there was no relief and none in sight. One local physician agreed to cover one night of call for $500. I took advantage of that twice. And then came a life preserver (mine). One of my residents from Bethesda Naval Hospital phoned and wanted to come and join my practice. Sweet hallelujah. Bob arrived with his wife, and because he'd been a student of mine I knew his skill set. He was a good surgeon. Not much of a personality, but what doctor does have one? The rules were simple and all in Bob's favor. He would pay nothing and be given half of the assets of the practice. He demanded Wednesdays off and no call on Saturdays. Why? Golf! It was all he knew and lived for. He was married, but his family took second place to Titleist golf balls. But now I had every other night off. As will come up in the future, years later (in 2002) after a number of medical disasters of mine related to Agent Orange, Bob brought in three other surgeons. Their pathology would fill a tome. My surgery schedule had decreased with the illnesses, but I ran the office and saw patients, referring the more difficult and hence higher-paying procedures to the partners. But as Granny said, "*Genug ist nicht genug.*" Enough is not enough. Yet stupidity reigned. I marketed the practice, gave them surgery cases, followed the patients post-op, and took a 60 percent pay loss. Sorry, not enough.

I came into the office one afternoon and was met by our corporate lawyer. We walked into our conference room where all of the docs sat. The offer was that I could leave my practice or they would leave. They knew that I couldn't cover the mortgage on the building I had built for them and pay our 18-member staff, who had become family to me. I looked at Dan our lawyer and at my 15-year partner, Bob. I said, "Is this really what you want, Bob? These others aren't even partners yet." He stared at the desk, would not look me in the eye, and said, "I can't argue, Tom, that with you gone, we could bring in another surgeon and double our salaries."

I stood still for who knows how long. My office manager stood at the end of the room crying. We loved each other and she took this move as hard as anyone. In two months she would leave the group and work for the hospital. I came back to sanity and, yes, I was raging, but calmer now than when I was a fighter pilot. I reached in my white coat and pulled out the front door key, tossing it on the table. "Best of luck, doctors. You deserve each other."

I never saw any of them again. But within four months, all four doctors were in a legal quagmire and went their separate ways. I didn't ask for financial remuneration and many have criticized me for that. Nonetheless, at the time, it simply felt right. Blood money, so to speak. Did any of them hear from our lawyer that I didn't want a penny and think, "My god, what did we *do*?" I doubt it, but I like to think so.

Where in the hell could I work? I headed to the V.A. and lasted 18 months. There was just too much pain, not melodrama, in trying to care for wounded vets and having crap available for them. "Hi, soldier. Looks like you'll need physical therapy and a muscle relaxant." Oh, no: We don't have a muscle relaxant because the government thinks you'll get addicted. And physical therapy is available only in Biloxi, Mississippi. A three-hour bus ride for 30 minutes of using rubber bands. It killed me. I left.

The V.A. can be a tremendous source of care for veterans and I have nothing but respect for the staff. I still use the V.A., augmented with civilian care, for my personal health needs. As with everything else in the government, you must pick and choose and know how to manipulate the system. My own V.A. doc, Mike Jacobs, is top-notch and truly cares. He makes me proud to have been there myself.

It was about this time, 2003, that life intended to keep the chaos of my life in a tailspin. I had spent much time and effort training in three other specialties. I did a fellowship in Obesity Medicine because so many of my patients suffered desperately from it and I felt ill-equipped to help. Pain Management was next in line and for the same reason as Obesity Medicine. And then somewhere along the path, I was hit by a thunderbolt: Disease was everywhere. Head and neck cancers. (I could operate on these patients all day for a ton of money.) Obesity and pain were ubiquitous, and family medicine was a critical need. It sounds so simple looking back at all of that, but I'm not the quickest racehorse in the stable. The question that kept battering my brain was the twenty-fifth letter of the alphabet, "Y." Why? Why the hell did all of this disease occur, and how in the hell could you prevent it? Pretty simple question and, as you'll see, a pretty simple answer. All disease, yes, all disease, stems from inflammation. It's that simple. Diabetes? Inflammation of the pancreas and receptor cell membranes. Coronary artery disease and hypertension? Inflammation of vascular walls. Cancer? Yup, inflammation of cellular DNA. And on it goes. So it didn't take long for me to decide that I needed to find the "why" of disease and the prevention. A formidable task, and, to the rescue, came my daughter Kristy. Kristy was in Colorado before going to medical school, and was working at a ski center.

"Hey, Dad, you need to come out and visit. I want you to meet this preventive medicine doctor, Ron Rothenberg, M.D." I was on my way in a heartbeat but I didn't know how many heartbeats I personally had left.

I met Ron and we became instant friends. I worked and studied with him. His San Diego practice was California Healthspan Institute and I came back to Pensacola to start Florida Healthspan Institute. We were a coast-to-coast twosome, but Ron was clearly the guru. I had much to learn and I committed to doing just that. What's the best weight-loss protocol? How to best treat post-op heart surgery patients? How can you quiet pain without using possibly addicting opiates? So many intriguing questions fascinated us and fueled our research. But there was a problem that naïve Tommy had never counted on. Ready?

Who wouldn't want to knock out pain, decrease cardiac disease, establish a paradigm of health and illness avoidance? We'd all love that, wouldn't we? We might, but hospitals and physicians don't. Why not? Eradicate illness and what are you going to fill the hospitals with? Perhaps Dollar General stores or condos with a pool, but there would be no reason for administrators, doctors, nurses, chefs, cleaners, and so on. Medicine is big business and from 10,000 feet, you need sick people to keep the cash flowing.

Consequently, hospitals had no interest in supporting our venture, and neither did insurance companies. If a patient was frustrated with the medical system they could see us, but had to pay out-of-pocket for labs, supplements, and care. The system is slowly changing, thanks to the outrage of patients toward the insurance companies. Add to that the fact that businesses have jumped on the supplement and magic-wand bandwagon. For example, there is a supplement called DHEA. Very real and very effective when used for the right purposes. We ordered ten bottles from ten companies. The bottles were labeled for, and had, 25-milligram tablets. When studied, nine of the bottles had no DHEA and were filled with sawdust, and one bottle had three milligrams. A total scam. How about a daily vitamin pill? Tons are sold daily. Evidence: They are of absolutely no help or advantage unless you're on a starvation diet. But they're flying off the shelves.

"But Doctor Schneider, they're only vitamins. They can't hurt." Really? It doesn't matter what the pill is; never, ever, never forget: Pills Kills. Last year we, doctors, in the U.S. killed 125,000 people because of medication errors, drug interactions, and plain stupidity. More about this later.

Chapter Sixteen

"What Goes Around Comes Around"

"Do things for people not for who they are or what they will return, but for who you are."

Every parent in America knows the most annoying nerve-wracking song ever composed. You'll sing it to yourself right now as you read this: "It's A Small World." Sorry for the reminder, but it really is a small world, and here's one example that shook my world.

I was working at my preventive-medicine clinic when the cell-phone rang, showing a call from San Diego, California. It was 2014 and my daughter was practicing psychiatry there, so I grabbed the phone a bit anxious that all might not be well. The male voice on the phone cooled the anxiety about my daughter, but I had no clue who was calling.

"Doctor T-bone Schneider, is that you?"

"Yes, it is. And who is this, please?"

"Captain, this is 'Ranger' Rick Risher. I was the rotor head [helo pilot] that pulled you out of the South China Sea 50 years ago."

His words flew at me with a slow southern drawl, but I still had no idea who he was. When I ejected, I was 22 scared shocked years old, and had no idea who had picked me up and flown me to the aircraft carrier. Turns out it was 'Ranger' Rick. He had logged of all his pickups and had kept the logbook all these years. Shortly after his tour in Vietnam, he left the Navy and became a civilian executive Learjet pilot, shuttling California celebrities around. Names like Arnie Palmer, Bob Hope, and a host of others were client names to him.

"Great to hear from you, Rick. I don't think I ever had the chance to formally thank you for the taxi ride back then. What can I do for you?"

Rick proceeded to tell me his medical horror show. He had been diagnosed with metastatic-to-bone prostate cancer. My heart sank. A tough diagnosis to deal with and battle. The more tragic aspect of his tale was that he was seen and diagnosed at the V.A. hospital in San Diego and the follow-up visit with the urologist was devastating. She told him that his cancer had spread to his spine and there was nothing that could be done. He had about three months to live. Now, that last phrase was all I needed to hear. I was back to my well-known mega-pissed mode. Three months? And how did you come up with that figure, Doctor god? Nobody predicts death. I explained that to Rick and said, "Rick, three letters: R-U-N!" And run he did. He was amazingly mature in his outlook. He was very religious and put his disease in god's hands and whatever could be done sanely he would do.

Rick flew to Pensacola where he was raised and his family still resided. Great. I called my old stomping ground, the V.A. Had him set for an appointment with the V.A. urologist as soon as Rick arrived. I met him after his appointment and my pissedness fumed to rage. The urologist agreed on three months and there was no treatment available. Rick was completely demoralized and depressed. He feigned his acceptance of his fate, but his dejection was palpable. I knew that aviation and his time in the Navy were pulsing in his blood and I needed an analogy that would spark light in his life.

"Hey, Rick, remember those sucky days in flight school when you begged yourself to quit? But you didn't. You just knew you'd make the next day better, didn't ya? Doesn't matter what the end would be, the perseverance was all that mattered. Damned if the bastards were gonna wear 'Ranger' down today! Well, here we go again, Rick. You, and I'll fly your wing, buddy."

Somehow that struck a chord for him. Maybe it was remembering the tough times in the Navy or maybe it was knowing he had a wingman. It doesn't really matter, because he was ready to fight, at least for today.

The next step was for me to get him to "caring." That meant buying tickets to MD Anderson Cancer Center. Rick was all in. He left and had a full workup with an extremely caring staff at Anderson. Scans, labs, physicals, and therapy. The whole course took nine months. That was four years ago. Once a month we have coffee and talk over old times together. I don't get to Pensacola often now, because we have moved to Chattanooga, Tennessee. But we do a Facetime coffee meeting all the same.

I still detest that Disney song, but it truly is a small world with some really serendipitous moments of joy.

Chapter Seventeen

Bring It On

"Although the world is full of suffering, it is also full of the overcoming of it."
-Helen Keller

Whenever I speak to a group on "wellness" I always preface my words with an apology to the audience. They will not hear about wellness per se, but rather I want to speak about something related to health. It's a word describing something harder to find today than Bin Laden used to be. Yes, you guessed it: TRUTH. So much pollution to swim through to get to truth, and then how do you know it's true? Should I listen to Oz and his miracle weight loss or Trump with his thought to drink Clorox to fight coronavirus? (Answer: Neither! And live to see another day.) Hey, come to think about it, why would you listen to me? (Answer: You shouldn't. You should research the information yourself. Check the National Institute of Health website, the CDC, PubMed and Medscape, all of which are highly respected. And don't forget your own doctor. Is he a member of my Three-A's club? Affability, availability, and ability.

And never forget that "doctor" means "teacher." Is he teaching you or only giving you pills?)

But here's a reason that you might want to at least look at my truth. I ask every audience to raise their hands with the following questions so I can get a feel for their well-being. Please raise your hand if you've had: hypertension (a few hands go up), gout, diabetes, Type 1 diabetes with insulin, cancer, perforated bowel, compressed vertebrae, renal failure needing dialysis, G.I. bleeding, have been 100 pounds overweight and lost it, sepsis (has an 85 percent mortality rate), pancreatitis, infected gallbladder, osteoarthritis, kidney stones, osteomyelitis (bacteria in bone), atrial fibrillation, abdominal abscesses, angina, three-vessel bypass heart surgery, five coronary stents (placed in Milan, Italy, by the inventor of stents, Dr. Antonio Colombo), and finally, has anyone mistaken a hearing aid battery for a pill (requires emergency surgery to remove)?

We could go on, but here's the real question. Please raise your hand if you've had all of those maladies and you're still alive?! And at every talk, one person has their hand up. Yup, that's me and my medical history. So the advice I give to patients is true because I've had to live it myself and I research medical facts daily. I'm not proud of my afflictions, but I've learned how to survive them and I want patients to take that home with them. No, I don't sell weight-loss pills or liver/colon cleansers. I sell the truth and it's free. I wrote most of the facts on preventive medicine and medical survival in a book, *A Physician's Apology*. Why an apology? Because unfortunately a great deal of what we as physicians expound is fraught with myths and errors.

I would be remiss if I did not comment on a few of my personal disasters. Many came from medical errors. For example, I was placed on Metformin for my diabetes. Totally appropriate and a daily occurrence today. Unfortunately, because of other meds I was taking, I developed a kidney stone. Off to the E.R. where a kidney study was done (IVP). I was drugged for the pain and whisked to radiology and given the dye and X-ray. The dye mixes with Metformin, and combined they try to kill your kidneys. I went into renal failure and had eight weeks of dialysis and meds to try and restore them. Voila. After eight weeks in ICU and losing 30 pounds, my kidneys came whimpering back to 40 percent of normal function. And here they sit today. How about a perforated bowel? Well, I was running triathlons and had achy knees. I was placed on Celebrex, a great anti-inflammatory. I gulped it down with a jigger of water and went on my run and bike workout. The pill sat in my small intestine and I was clearly dehydrated. Whammo, the perfect setup for the pill to erode its way through my intestines. Cost? Ten weeks in the ICU with nothing by mouth. All nutrients given intravenously. Mark and Kristy visited the Navy hospital every day and put stickers of hamburgers and French fries on the I.V. bag. Forty pounds down and eight weeks later, I was home. My motto: Medicines are needed and save lives at times, *but* Pills Kills.

That list of illnesses occurred from 1994 thru 2012. During that time, a number of devastating social events took their toll. First, as mentioned, my practice of four physicians and a partner decided they needed me gone and they wanted to bring in another money-making surgeon. As mentioned, I left tacitly and they ended up suing each other within six months of my leaving. My ex-wife Diane and I divorced and it was tantamount to Gettysburg in the Civil War. Happily, all of that has passed now. I met Merrill during that time and within a year we were married, twice. Why twice?

Well, my angina heart problem was flaring up and it was determined that I needed stents. Unfortunately, the stents I needed were not available for diabetics in the U.S. I contacted the guru in Milan, Italy (Dr. Colombo), and he assured me that he could help. Merrill and I sold most of our belongings and headed for Venice. I surprised Merrill by taking her to St. Mark's Cathedral and bringing her up to the altar and reciting vows. I remember them today. (I honor the divine that is you, and you honor the divine that is me, and in this way, we are one.)

I was so short of breath I barely got the words out, but I remember that hundreds of visitors to the cathedral that morning stopped, looked at us with oohs and ahhs, applauding as we finished. Now "divine, please" get me to Milan!

Dr. Colombo precisely placed five coronary stents in me using no anesthesia. Each stent placement felt like a heart attack because they must block off the heart's blood, like a heart attack. The pain beat me after the fourth stent. I passed out. That's a lousy way to have the effect of anesthesia, but I'll take it. I left the next day for Florence by train with Merrill. The Florence train station said there were no seats left on the train back to Milan. Time for a lie. I went to the ticketmaster and I pointed to exhausted Merrill and explained that my wife had severe cancer and was needed in Milan for her chemotherapy. He graciously bumped two passengers and gave us their seats. To this day I feel guilty and full of remorse. Oh, sorry, no, I don't. The short story is that we arrived in the Monet-painted city and I climbed the 463 stairs of the Duomo cathedral. No shortness of breath. Stents: I like you. Dr. Colombo: I thank you! Merrill, I love you. Fifteen years later, the stents remain open and I send Dr. Antonio Colombo a yearly thank you. And for the religious, yes, Merrill and I remarried in Colorado legally after we returned to the States.

On the way home, Merrill and I were exhausted but happy and relieved. And as we flew over the United States, I looked out of the plane and, through the clouds, could see the Grand Canyon below. I pointed it out to Merrill and she mentioned how much she wanted to visit. Had I ever been there? I said that I had been there multiple times and, once, it burned me. The story was that after returning from Vietnam I was asked to fly a Navy jet from San Diego to Naval Air Station Fallon in Nevada. Fallon was a base used to practice gunnery and bombing runs. I would fly in one aircraft and another young pilot would fly wing on me. All went well and it was a "cake" flight, but as we crossed over the Grand Canyon, I asked the other pilot if he'd seen the Canyon up close. His response was "No." Okay, then it's tour time. We dove down and scurried through the Canyon jinxing left and right through the turns. It must have been a mini air show for the Canyon visitors.

Landing in Fallon, as we taxied in, two Shore Patrol police vehicles approached. Naturally I thought this was customary deference to visiting pilots. But why would my "life script" change now? The Shore Patrol took us to the Ops office where we were severely reprimanded for flying through the sacred Hopi Indian burial grounds. There is only one short segment where helos can transport visitors to the bottom of the Canyon. All else is a federal flight violation. Naturally! We were escorted to the bachelor officer quarters in house-arrest confinement for a week. But that's not the end of the Grand Canyon for me. Merrill sat back in her seat next to me in the 737 and sighed, whispering, "How are you still alive?" Not sure I was supposed to hear that.

A few years later, in 2004, Merrill and I were married and surviving my litany of medical disasters. Our divorces were finalized and the only spur in our families remained her son. He was graduating from high school, angry at the world, uninterested in academics, and he despised me, which was also encouraged by his outré father. Her son had not grown up with discipline and I represented the "Führer."

Merrill decided that a trip to the Grand Canyon would be a real treat for her son and a classmate friend of his. Fine. Off we went.

I have a bad habit left over from the Jesuits. I ask of anyone who will listen questions that have no fixed answer. What is truth, what is our purpose, what are your guidelines of life, and many more. Of course teenagers love this probing! Maybe not? Just ask my children. Merrill's son had a particular distaste for my questions, but his best friend, Greg, loved them. Greg asked if I had ever been to the Canyon before and I told him the story of flying through it and the punishment. He loved the story, but Merrill's son said, "Don't believe a word he says; he's full of sh--!" I replied, "Believe as you wish, but always look for the truth."

Okay, that set the tone of the trip. Quite a thrill ride for me. But here's the thing: Sometimes karma is real. In this case it couldn't have been better scripted. Greg asked me for my meaning of life and I told him he'd know before the trip ended, but he'd have to work for it. Merrill's son simply said, "Keep it, I don't want it." Fine.

The next day after settling in at the hotel on the Grand Canyon, Merrill asked if we could go to the bottom. I knew they'd never make the walk down and back in one day and I was damned if I was going to take the mule ride down and back. I respect my hemorrhoids too much. So how about a helicopter ride? All were excitedly in favor. Tickets were bought and off we went. Everyone was Disneyland jazzed and thrilled by the flight down to the bottom. How can you not be ecstatic with that view? Truly spectacular, it fills all with awe. We landed and walked to a boat ramp where "Indian Joe," a Hopi Indian, was waiting with a motorboat to take us a mile down the river. Indian Joe was right off an MGM movie set. He wore an Indian wide-brimmed hat with two feathers nodding from a headband made of turquoise and white stones. Unshaven and with well-worn knee-high moccasins, he gave a canned history of the Canyon. He really had his heart in his history, regardless of the time he spent putting up with cellular-camera-laden tourists. And then it happened. Karma. It loses its ecstasy in the translation, but this came as true as real.

Joe tossed an anchor and we all just sat, listened, and enjoyed. No one spoke until Merrill's son said the obvious: "Man, it's so quiet down here." Indian Joe looked at him and, after a pause, said, "Always quiet. Our sacred site. But many, many years ago, not so quiet. Two Navy jets flew by, awakening our sacred grounds. Pilots caught and put in jail." He spoke broken English with a Hopi accent. Holy Lone Ranger and Tonto. Merrill, her son, and Greg had faces that reminded me of the Edvard Munch painting "The Scream." Merrill's eyes said to the boys, "Not one word or I swear I'll throw you into the river." Unbelievable but true. I couldn't have paid enough to have that staged. Merrill's son Robert never expressed to me another doubt.

We headed back to the helicopter in silence. And as we walked the shoreline, I picked up two flat skipping rocks. But they weren't for skipping. Later in the trip I scraped on each rock's surface "YBM." On the way home from the Canyon, I gave each boy the rock and told them that was one of my life guides. After lots of begging on Greg's part, I explained that the letters stood for "You Before Me," in all things. This motto had never failed me and was just another reminder of how much of a guidepost kindness would be in my life, for the rest of my life. Now here's the amazing payback. What are two teenage boys going to do with that? Probably throw the rocks as skipping stones. But many years later, Merrill's son married, and his best friend Greg naturally attended the wedding. I hadn't seen Greg in many years. He came up to me in the crowd of wedding guests and told me about his successful career and life. "Hey, Greg," I said, "do you remember that Grand Canyon trip?" "Of course I do, sir. It was life-changing for me. And Robert and I always end our emails with 'YBM' to this day." I couldn't help it. I teared right up. Inertia at work.

The Canyon had more to offer on that trip, life-changing for many. Of course the Grand Canyon is completely indescribable. Approach it for the first time and expect to lose your breath. It is that inspiring. The colors, the shapes, the enormity and sheer beauty are—sorry, I'm not following what I said about its being indescribable. Only room for one place on a bucket list? The Grand Canyon. And during this trip, Merrill experienced all of that. It brought her to that magical place of dreams and wishes, with a touch of euphoria. Even the nights at the Grand Canyon are spectacular. The stars are never brighter or more numerous. You are immediately transported to an understanding of your humble insignificance in our universe. It was during one of Merrill's and my night walks along the rim that it happened. A group of three- to five-year-olds were walking hand in hand with their parents and Merrill stopped to watch. Moments of silence, and then she turned to me and said, "If

I had any wish, it would be to have raised a child with you." I knew the feeling and was touched deeply by the idea. It took me about a second to reply, "It's not too late. Let's do it!"

Suddenly Merrill had panic and concern on her face. "It would have to be an immaculate conception. I've had a hysterectomy and I'm 50. How could it possibly happen?"

Without a pause, I blurted, "Adoption!" I could see that she realized I was serious, and the thought set off her well-founded trepidation. We continued to talk and I thoroughly understood her concerns, but there was a touch of excitement in her words as well. We ended our walk in a small log-cabin grocery along the rim. Gum, goodies, and sunscreen to the checkout. Then Merrill headed back to the magazine rack to pick up something to read. I stood dutifully at the counter waiting to pay. On the counter was a rack of laminated sheets filled with those saccharine phrases like, "Today is the first day of the rest of your life." Yuck! Not for me, but I thumbed through them to waste time. I came across one that was a full page long and I pulled it out to read. It was a parable of a well-dressed businessman near a beach seeing an elderly woman walking along the shore, bending down and picking up starfish and tossing them back into the waves. The shore was littered with these starfish, so the man felt empathy for the woman and approached her. As she continued to bend and toss he said to her, "Ma'am, this beach is miles long with thousands of starfish. I'm sorry, but you can't really make a difference." The woman simply bent down, picked up another starfish and tossed it. She looked at the man and said quietly, "I made a difference to that one."

Now I'm not much for mystical messages, but how do you dismiss that? "Merrill, please take a look at this." Merrill came over, read the story, and started to cry. I looked at her tears and said, "I think we're looking for our starfish." Little did we know how difficult that search would be.

Chaos! Only that word describes our next two years of an adoption roller coaster. But roller coasters can be fun and there was not an ounce of fun in looking for our "starfish." We didn't qualify to adopt from the U.S. because of our age. I still had connections in the State Department from my military days. China was our only hope. We were referred to Fei Yang, an adoption facilitator. I learned early on that the Chinese government was going to be a formidable adversary and I would have to resort to deceit and lies. I felt so guilty—oh, er, no, I didn't. Fei was tremendous in guiding us through the gauntlet, explaining early on that China wanted any adopting parents to have a spotless medical history including colds. Absurd? Yes, but all part of the game. We found our starfish online in a Chinese orphanage, although orphanage is not the word for the hellhole that these children lived in. Twelve hundred children and four nannies to care for them, infants and up to ten years old. After that, the girls are sent for prostitution or to work in factories making blue jeans for 16 hours a day. It is heartbreaking to see and impossible to understand.

When Merrill and I saw the situation in China, it reminded me of Vietnam. The sight of wounded and burned children in Vietnam is cauterized into my dreams. Seeing the orphanage in China was as devastating. The environment that our starfish was in was stark. No toys or teaching, and nutrition was a water soup with greens and very little protein. We chose our daughter, who had been abandoned at birth and placed in a train station. She had cigarette burns on her abdomen and was severely malnourished and had scabies. Her bed in the orphanage was made of bamboo slats on a dirt floor. Her name was Xiuling. It means, translated, "gentle and beautiful," and indeed she was. We added "Eleanor" as her name to continue Merrill's family-heirloom legacy name. She was three years old and was now the eighth Eleanor in Merrill's family history.

There were many up and downs in the year and a half prior to leaving for China to pick up "Ellie." China demanded many thousands of dollars in uncirculated bills. We underwent three "in house" exams and inspections. The Chinese government investigated every aspect of our lives and the U.S. government wasn't any smoother. Ellie was to become a 100 percent U.S. citizen, renouncing her Chinese government status, and 100 percent our daughter. Paperwork galore and never-ending. Most of the tedious data collecting and paperwork was done by Merrill and it definitely took its toll on her. Weekly fluctuations were nerve-wracking. "Yes, you're moving ahead in the process," to "No, wrong paperwork or needing a better physical exam." The physical exam required pure deception. Call me David Copperfield! I have filled out more than one physical-examination form. My filled-out fake form had me as healthy as Schwarzenegger. It took some practice for the signing doctor's signature to look official, but fortunately most doctors have the writing skills of a three-year-old. The U.S. government and China bought it. What does that tell you about security? My real medical history would fill a medical student's textbook, but that's certainly not a book I wanted the governments to read. We needed to toss our starfish into the ocean of a family.

Merrill and I left for six weeks in China, which was China's requirement. Fei came with us and was enormously helpful. We did the usual tourist things to fulfill our requirement, but of course our thoughts and interests were totally focused on Ellie. How would she react? Was she healthy? Did I bring enough medicines to treat her? Questions came by the minute, but we finally met her at the consulate's office and she took our hands and started walking toward the door. Of course she spoke no English and my Chinese was pathetic. Merrill and I simply kept repeating the Chinese for "mama" and "daddy" and "I love you." And the most amazing aspect of the entire process was how amazingly Ellie adapted to her new parents. From the moment we left the consulate, Ellie melted into "Mom" and "Dad." It truly was as if she had been born that day. We were a bona fide family, meant to be, and this has never wavered.

Returning home was a piece of cake. And here's the takeaway. Ellie spoke not a word of English, had never been loved by parents, had never seen a grown man or a dog, had never drawn with crayons. McDonald's, cars, snow, a bed? She dove immediately into all of life as we know it. Three days after arriving home in Pensacola, Florida, we enrolled her in Montessori pre-school. Nine years later, she graduated the eighth grade as her class valedictorian. She started in the International Baccalaureate program at Pensacola High School, a highly selective academic program. My older two children, now both physicians, had also attended that program and we were very confident about its academics. Mark and Kristy had tightly bonded with their new sister and they encouraged and advised Ellie. Kristy had two daughters of her own and Mark had a son. Yup, this was a thriving family and life was flowing. But wait a second, please, because we're chatting about me. Sure, I've had about every disease known to man, but that wasn't a hurdle I couldn't overcome. Remember my mantra that "Pills Kills"? I still needed to make the point. I was placed on a weekly injection of a medicine that would help to boost insulin for my diabetes. Great drug and very effective, but its side effect, although rare, could be devastating.

After four months on the medication and with Ellie at age eight, I awoke one morning with excruciating abdominal pain. The emergency room physician evaluated labs and told me to go home and stop drinking because I had pancreatitis. In a stupor of pain, I explained that I hadn't had alcohol in 40 years. "Sure, sure, Captain. Home will be best for you." I made it at home for about four hours and then Merrill found me in bed stuporous and incoherent. She somehow managed to take me to our local hospital where the staff knew me from my medical and surgical practice. The physicians agreed to admit me for pancreatitis, but the process didn't work as it does on TV shows. I was placed in a wheelchair to wait for a hospital bed to be readied. Two and a half hours later I collapsed onto the floor. By the grace of Confucius, a dear physician friend, Dr. Norm Haines, came by and found me. He examined me, yelled for a stretcher, and ordered me brought to the ICU, to be given I.V.s, intubated on a ventilator, catheterized, and surrounded by monitors galore. I had been in this position many times before from other diseases as sequelae of Agent Orange. You'd think I would be a pro. Somehow or other, I never learned to enjoy any of it. No other words besides "It sucked." After days went by, the diagnosis was sepsis. This is an infection that has extended to every part of your body. It beats up every organ system, such as heart, kidney, lungs, and brain. It has an 85 percent mortality rate. Mark and Kristy were advised to fly in for a fond farewell to dear old Dad. But no, that was not to be my path. They found six abscesses in my abdomen and my dear friend Dr. Hank Cramer put six drains into my abdomen through my skin. Surprisingly, I didn't find that enjoyable either! I was on three antibiotics with no success. My infectious-disease physician gave a dire prognosis to my family and none of that bothered me. Why? Because I was in a comatose state and never heard a word. He said that he could try a cancer chemo therapeutic drug, but it would be a shot in the dark. Nice aiming, Doc! My temperature came down and my blood picture improved. My head status was still off track, but my family would testify that I have always been a few degrees off on a different railroad. They still laugh at an episode that occurred after I had improved medically. They helped walk me to the bathroom for obvious reasons, but as I reached the door I began refusing to go in, stomping my feet and yelling, "Kill them, kill them!" They thought I was having a Vietnam flashback and told me I wasn't in the war. I kept yelling about the thousands of spiders in the bathroom climbing up my leg. Finally they told me to pee on the spiders and they'd leave. So I did. I don't remember any of it, but to this day I feel very badly for the orderly assigned then to clean my room. And after seven weeks in the ICU, I was discharged home on an antibiotic cocktail that Merrill injected into my central I.V. every morning and night. Eight weeks later I was free, up and walking and eating. But I was one limp dish rag. It would take a full year of exercise, walking, rowing, and weight training before I was fully functional. Ellie thus had her first education about the frailty of life and her dad's PPP (piss-poor protoplasm). My practice had been closed, and my interactions with patients were pro bono and by phone.

That still holds true today. And if every disaster is a learning opportunity, here's what I've learned:

Showers are like being in heaven.
There's always someone worse off than I.
Mashed potatoes and gravy, mmm!
Nothing beats sleep.
A touch is better than any pill.
Breathe fresh air and smile every day.
It's not all about me!
Crying is okay and good for me.
YBM=You Before Me.
Water is my life blood.
My mind is my best physician.
Giving compliments makes me smile.
Pills Kills.
Exercise every day.
Anger is the real heart killer.
Think you can or can't, and you're right.
In the end, only kindness matters.

I swear that those lines could probably be in some country-and-western songs because they're so trite, but so help me, they pump through my veins every day. Life, giving, and kindness are all that really matter.

Chapter Eighteen

What's In It for You?

"What matters is how well you laugh, how well you give, and how well you let go"

How rude of me to think that you've come all this way just for the stories. I mentioned that the word "doctor" means teacher, and I must adhere to that title. This is not meant to pontificate, but simply to help you avoid your future potholes.

Learning and education can come in various forms. But the old adage that education is an expensive proposition is true. The expense is not necessarily in financial loss. The more costly aspect is the time, emotional pain, and stress costs. We can learn by experience, as I have, or learn through educational media. Learning from others' experiences is clearly the easier route. Perhaps not as indelible as your own personal experiences, but learning from others is clearly less painful. I have never been pregnant (probably one of the only medical conditions I haven't had) but my abdominal diseases have given me incredible empathy for every childbirth. I would have preferred to read about it in "Mother's Daily," but learning is all that matters. Perhaps you'll learn how to avoid your pitfalls and remember how to cope when they occur. Yes, "when" they occur. Because they will for sure. We are all here to give and enjoy and then die. And unfortunately not all of us will die quietly while sleeping at 3:00 in the morning. Again, I will not "pass" when I die, but I will die. If I develop an injury suddenly, like the broken foot I now have, I am reminded of a phrase my son said 26 years ago. It will sound like a hackneyed sentiment on a Hallmark card, but it is truer than any thought that passes my mind.

It happened after a triathlon I did in 1994. During the final phase, the run, I noticed that my left shoulder was aching, and as I've mentioned, when I was evaluated the next day my signs and symptoms warranted a cardiac catheterization. The cath confirmed major coronary plaques, and cardiac bypass surgery would be required. When? Tomorrow morning, came the reply, and we are admitting you to the hospital now. The surgery in those days was still relatively new and I was a tad apprehensive. What could calm me down? I started daydreaming about coming aboard an aircraft carrier at night in the rain. Catching the three wire and peeing in my flight suit. Bypass? What a piece of cake. The other thought I used while lying in the hospital bed was that it wasn't happening at that moment. I was lying comfortably in bed, without pain. I remembered my grandmother's words, "Don't waste your tears on tomorrow." I remember friends coming by to wish me well. I told them to please save their wishes for my surgeon and nurses, because I'd be asleep for all of it, provided the anesthesia worked!

When I awakened from the surgery, I was in the cardiac ICU with a party of nurses around my bed. Most of them I had known quite well and I had flirted with all of them. Polite sincere flirting, by the way, pays off in dividends a hundredfold. All I remember was choking on a tube that was breathing for me and feeling enormous pain in my chest from the bone-splitting incision. I kept watching the respirator pulsing up and down as it forced oxygen into my lungs. Each pulse of breath expanded my chest and thus pulled at my chest incision. I was miserable, unable to speak, and trying to sync into the ventilator's rhythm. And then I felt it. Weird. But my right big toe was being squeezed firmly. Then a whisper in my ear in a voice I knew as well as my own, "This too shall pass, Dad." My son Mark had weaseled his way into the ICU (flirting with the nurses) and came to my bedside. To this day, I never forget those words or that squeeze. "This too shall pass." And here's the thing, it does! It has! And it will continue! Words that have pulled my thinking through many a disaster. I highly recommend it as a prescription.

Mark had left college when he heard about the surgery and proceeded to stay at home rehabbing me for a year. We walked the beach and he gave me exercises to slowly recover. At the end of the year, we goaled to complete a triathlon. I think it must have taken me a week to finish it. (Not really, but yes, ten hours.) Mark stayed with me to the end although he probably could have won it. Shortly after that, he joined the Navy and life went on. When he left, it was one of the saddest days of my life. I spent many of the following days crying at the beach. Yes, I missed my two children, and that hasn't changed in 24 years. We still try to chat every day. And now with Ellie, three amazing adults who have made my life the best ever. I wouldn't change a day! And I will nominate for Nobel Prizes Diane and Merrill, without whom I would not have survived my various medical catastrophes. This too shall pass. They carried the banner.

Here's a cute teaching aphorism: "Look before you leap." I learned it slightly differently. It went like this. I was working in an indigent free clinic in the inner city. One of my goals was to get patients walking, so what better way than with a pedometer. I bought a large box of old pedometers and found their batteries useless. No problem. I took out one of the small round batteries that was covered in white plastic. I would get new ones that size. I put the battery in my breast pocket. Unfortunately, I had put my diabetes drug, metformin, into that pocket earlier, to take later.

Heading home by car, I remembered that I needed to take my metformin pill. Easy fix, as I had water with me. Eyes on the road, reach into my pocket, see that it's white, and plop-plop fizz-fizz down went the "pill." When I was home, I reached in to check the battery and, well, you know the rest. My pill was in my hand and my battery was in my intestines. Now as a doctor, perhaps a goofy one as my daughter says, I did know that this was now an emergency. If gastric juices opened the battery, it would perforate my intestines (again!). Been there done that, so I raced to my G.I. doc, Dr. Haines, and the X-ray showed the battery nestled in my colon. I was given gallons of liquid laxatives to get the critter out the back door. Only one problem. It was Wednesday, and Merrill, Ellie, and I were scheduled to leave for Europe on Friday. Uh-oh. If the battery wasn't out by Friday morning, the trip that had been planned for a year would be canceled. Need I mention how thrilled Merrill was with this predicament? Well, by Thursday afternoon it was still in my lower colon. A recheck on Friday was not better. Norm elected to zonk me with anesthesia and remove it by colonoscopy. Success! Norm came into the recovery room and said he had been successful but concerned because he also found this. What? He had put a "D" battery (the monster) in a specimen container. Even drugged, I laughed until I peed. He asked if I take the batteries for preventive medicine or with a side salad. I squeaked out a reply of "No, Norm, I just really get a 'charge' out them." It was the best trip overseas I've ever had since the anesthesia kept me down until arrival. I have no idea how Merrill put me on the plane. As you can imagine, Ellie seldom lets a day go by without mentioning my dietary boo-boo. Youth can be so cruel. Now I look before I swallow.

The battery of course will cause inflammation if not removed, but it is a reminder that ALL diseases are caused by inflammation (in my case, add stupidity). Diabetes, for example, is inflammation of the pancreas, hypertension is inflammation of the arterial walls, and even cancer starts as inflammation of the nucleus of the cell. So the real question for us when we develop a disease is "Why?" It's not "Which pill do I take?" And it's important to remember that we instigate a large percentage of the inflammation. How? We eat too much sugar and alcohol, yielding acid. Too much food in general causes obesity that secretes more inflammation. Too little sleep and too much anger will beat us up horribly. Did I mention smoking (any kind)? Don't waste the money. Just suck on a flame thrower! Of course the list is endless and frankly I love things like Snickers, popcorn, and Cheetos. Give them up? Not on my life! (No pun intended.) We need to listen to Socrates: Everything in moderation. If I die with a mouthful of ice cream, then it's been a good life. My motto is "once in a while." That translates to ice cream once a week for me, adding a tad more insulin to compensate. Well worth it, in my opinion.

I started with "What's in it for you?" And perhaps another full book might deal with what to take away from a life with so many bumps in the road. But the one aspect that kept rearing its nasty head was the selfish gene in me and perhaps you. How can

I find "happy" and how do I find enjoyment in the midst of crisis and chaos? Granted, those are tough questions and everyone needs to find their own answers, but it's a killer trying to find the panacea when you're in pain or stressed. I sure as hell don't have all the answers, but I've had enough experience to know what works. I have a mnemonic that I use the moment I hit disaster and it has been an anesthetic for me in my life. We spoke about "This too shall pass," and I have mumbled it over and over a thousand tears during my life. And yes, it works as a truthful mantra. But to put it all together and find happiness and enjoyment, my go-to is "GAGE." Heck, even I can remember that one. It goes like this: "G" stands for "gratitude." Every chance you get each day you need to love yourself enough to be thankful. Thankful for life, for having a broken foot that's not needing a prosthesis, or having a prosthesis and being thankful for life and seeing the absolute gorgeous beauty of nature. And how about the smell of breakfast? Countless things to be thankful for. We need only to see and count them every day. The "A" is my really tough one and I'd be lying if I didn't say how difficult it is for me. It represents "acceptance," accepting what comes your way, good or bad. If it's a good day, accept and be grateful, not arrogant or cocky. You don't deserve it, it's just life happening. If it's a bad day, great, another opportunity to show your strength. You don't deserve it that day. Tough. Nobody cares. It's just life happening. Suck it up, buttercup. It's an opportunity to give and strengthen.

The next "G" is for "giving." Give what? Everything if you're a saint, but most of us don't reach Mother Teresa status. But we can give to others in a never-ending way. Put your checkbook away. Do the charitable giving on your own schedule. I'm talking about giving to the unseen. That's the gal cashier from the grocery. She hears beep-beep as the food passes all day. She says, "Sir, did you find everything alright?" I reply, "Thanks, but no. I didn't find the lottery numbers or a blue blazer, size 44 extra-long." And then I end with, "Thanks so much. You did a great job." I vary it every day to the point where my wife and daughter won't go through the check-out line with me anymore. But I have yet to not get a smile from each checker. Who wins on that deal? Me, of course. Giving one smile made a difference to her. Or even walking in the park and passing someone who says briefly, "How are you?" I reply, "Better for seeing you. Never better." You get it. Giving to others will make your life a joy. And, by the way, we're all the "others," all of us "unseen."

Oh, the "E"? "E" is for enjoyment/happiness. How does that work? Well, here's a promise. Practice G-A-G every day and you will live in E. I've never found anything that works as well. It will bring you smiles, or has it already?

Chapter Nineteen

Neither You Nor I'm to Blame, When All Is Said and Done

"Life is peaceful and melodic when you can see the good in others."
-Me

What is the meaning of life? I don't care. It's tough enough trying to have life full of meaning.

This has been an erratic and amazing journey and as they say in the Bronx, "It ain't over yet!" I must admit that over the years I've wondered why I'm not dead. I wonder what is my purpose, and all of the other questions that all of us who stop and think for a moment ask ourselves. But as with all difficult questions, I too tend to put the questions away for the day. They re-emerge during those quiet times of being alone, perhaps even a tad sad. What am I doing? Why am I doing it? How did I get here? Perhaps these are some of the real questions we need to grapple with. The answer to "What will I have for dinner?" isn't going to make a huge change in my life. "How did I get here?" is game-changing, along with "Where am I going?"

Somewhere among those musings I have had to come up with internal guides to keep me on my hidden path and add a hold on sanity. This was brought to the forefront for me while writing this.

I don't know how to classify the incident, but it probably doesn't need categorizing. Here's what happened.

A hot afternoon, midsummer in Chattanooga, 2020, and I was bemoaning my broken foot and inability to enjoy the simple pleasures of life. No driving the car and no walking the dog. If I needed anything while sitting on the sofa, it required a "Hey, Ellie, can I trouble you for. . .?" or "Merrill, may I bother you for. . .?" So frustrating. The self-pity was interrupted by my cellphone's ring. It was a long-ago friend of mine calling to ask for medical advice. The calls for advice have become a daily ritual in today's medical climate. Patients can't reach their doctor or have their questions answered; a simple query would require an appointment. I guess that's why medicine today is oftentimes "fee for service." Hey, how about a doctor who will answer your questions for free? Now there's an idea, although not a profitable one. But what idiot doctor is going to do that? Okay, me. Doctors have asked me about the malpractice risk. Well, here's the thing. I haven't ever been sued. Patients appreciate everything you can do for them, particularly when there's no financial incentive. And lastly, go ahead and sue me. I purchased a Honda in 2003 and it just recently blew up on the highway. No injuries, but also, now, no car. I have a simple life that translates to lawyers as: What possible good is it to sue him? He doesn't even have malpractice insurance!

Sorry; back to the phone call. After coming up with a game plan for my caller, D., she switched gears on me and asked a probing question I was barely ready to answer. She mentioned that she had read my previous book, *A Physician's Apology*. In it I described in detail some of the medical disasters that occurred with me. She had listened to me speak and couldn't believe that so much bad luck could happen to one person. Was it really all true? Was there more to the story? And can anyone survive all that? My immediate phone response was "Yes, yes, and yes."

The question prompted some serious soul-searching (how's that for alliteration?) on my part. I think all of us have times when mandatory introspection hits us and we must define who we are and why. I've had hundreds of such times, but without ever having that "Aha!" moment of fully understanding.

The best that I've come up has become a minor creed of mine. And the first theme of the creed comes down to one goal. It grew from a question to me about longevity. How do you live longer? My answer is that the real goal is to live better. If longer happens, great, but there's no magic pill for that. Fish oil? Organic foods? No, it's even simpler. As a base, you must *want* to live longer. Without that basic desire, it ain't gonna happen. The goal of a healthy life is, of course, up to you. Still want to do marathons, but your arthritis is vicious? Two choices: Get comfy in that big easy chair, or switch to swimming or walking or a rowing machine. You might want to throw in a book now and then to keep the upstairs moving. We just adapt and adjust. And often, it's a choice. There's the old story of the 80-year-old wife who turned to her 85-year-old husband and said, "Honey, let's go upstairs and make crazy love." He looked kindly at her and said, "Sorry, honey, but pick one. I can only do one of those." Yup, safe choices.

Resilience is another must-have. Webster defines it as the ability of a body to recover from or adjust to misfortune or change. Here's the thing: Life is misfortune and change. The size varies from person to person, but we all get to carry the load sometimes. I have recently been diagnosed with rheumatoid arthritis and there isn't a time when some part of me isn't saying "Sit down!" Do I have to get on the rowing machine? You bet. As with childhood beatings, you learn to say "Bring it on, but don't expect this to bring me down." But wait a second. I really hurt and this isn't going away. Poor me. Guess what? Wait for it—nobody cares! That's right. Oh, they feel sorry for you having your dilemma, but of more importance is the fact that they don't have it! People aren't mean; they're just human. I first learned this from a book written by a nurse. I read it after my bypass surgery, and if I could recall the title and author today, I'd send her flowers. She wrote about all the healthy things to do for your heart from a diet and exercise standpoint. As a physician and wellness researcher, most of the information was known to me and it served as a great reminder. But as I read on, she made critical points that I've never forgotten. First, she said that now that I've had bypass surgery, I must realize that I'm not "fixed." I received only a Band-Aid. That's right, a Band-Aid. The disease continues. What about the "Why did I have this disease?" It took years for me to understand that the effects of anger, Agent Orange, lifestyle, and stress were major clues to the "Why?" She went on to say that the recovery and prevention of persistent disease was my responsibility and not my doctor's and not my pill case's. The final point was the tip of the sword for me. She reminded me that in three to six months, everyone would forget that I had had heart surgery. But I could never let myself forget. Life as I knew it must change. Easy. Not on my life (pun intended)! I had to prioritize my lifestyle choices. Meditation? Slowing down, pouring ice water on my white-hot embers of anger. So much to learn, but resilience was going to be my new middle name. I would need that resilience for all of the illnesses to come. Regardless of the disease and pain, I pumped through my veins "This too shall pass," "Bring it on," and "I will and want to live through this." Thanks for the cards and flowers, folks, but I've just got to suck it up. Hey, Russ, can you hear me? Go ahead with one more belt whipping. I double-dog-dare you!

Persistence was next on my mantra. I don't know how Webster defines it, but my son Mark and daughters Kris and Ellie are the embodiment of it. For example, my son hit every wall imaginable trying to get into medical school. He took the admissions test six times. So depressing. But the result was success and an M.D. For Kris, it was an M.D. and working through not one but two residencies, in Family Medicine and Psychiatry. Ellie lives with and manages chronic hepatitis B carried from China. On a daily basis, she ensures her health and well-being and lives as the paragon of fitness. I remember giving my son a plaque upon his graduation from medical school. In Latin it read *ter quater surgere cadent*—fall down three times, stand up four.

Now what helps keep those principles alive in tough times? This woman had the answer. Her name was Udae. She was 101 years old, living in Okinawa. I met her on a medical "help" trip. This was in 1998 and Okinawa had a record number of centenarians. Udae was kind enough to answer my questions. Naturally, "What keeps you so young?" was tops on my list. Her day involved waking at sunrise, a vegetarian breakfast with tea, caring for her garden, and then a half-mile walk to her daughter's hut to manage the garden there. Her daughter was riddled with arthritis so "Mom" did the gardening. There's the definition of "family."

I asked Udae what gave her energy every day. What kept her smiling on bad days? She didn't even blink. "Ikigai." There is no adequate translation from the Japanese, but it essentially means a "daily giving passion" within yourself. She expounded that the giving is a "kindness" in the day. Giving and kindness. Not as a tag line or bumper sticker, not merely a Sunday sermon. This is a moment-to-moment passion that is as real as her breath. When you think about it, those principles of life are not mystical or esoteric. We have had prophets galore who, when asked "How do we best live?" always answered so poignantly, "Do unto others as you would have done unto yourself." Kindness to others and kindness to yourself. Do you think that might actually work? I'll ask Udae and get back to you.

Who would deny that these principles are purely selfish? Yes, they guarantee far more getting for the giver than for the getter. But I would be remiss if I didn't mention another principle that I only recently had emotionally driven into my core. Here's what happened.

A tad of background: After my divorce from Diane, I repeatedly asked for one thing. I craved photographs of my children when they were young. I knew that we had hundreds and Diane was a neatnik and had categorized every one. The answer was always no. Fifteen years of "no" and I gave up trying. Then, she was recently diagnosed with cancer. Surgery, radiation, and chemotherapy. I went to her biopsy and kept in touch regarding recovery. And a few weeks ago, it happened. I received a shoebox-sized package in the mail. I could tell from the addressing that the handwriting was Diane's. The other giveaway was the smell. Musty, mossy, moldy, wafted from the box. At least 16 years in storage. Opening the lid, I was filled with boyish excitement. Like Christmas morning and finding a Red Rider BB gun under the tree in the movie *A Christmas Story*. At least 750 photos were neatly tucked in the box. There was even protective bubble wrap lining the box. And like someone racing through the winning lottery numbers, I flipped through each one. Teary? Yes, but I think it must have been an allergy to the mold. How could what seemed like a million years of photo history get me so welly?

As I flipped to the next picture, excited that each picture was more elating than the one before, I fingered a laminated card. It was larger than the other pictures and although laminated the picture quality was faded. My breath left me suddenly. It was a photo of my brother Mark. Mark died on September 29, 1968. But he has never left my being. I still talk to him, and although I would be admitted to a psych ward for admitting that, I'm reminded of a line in the movie *Oh, God!* At the end of the movie, John Denver asks God as he heads away into the clouds, "Can we still talk, God?" George Burns as God replies, "Tell you what, sonny. You talk and I'll listen." Best theology line ever. And I guess that's how I think of Mark. He never spoke a single word during his life and yet he said so much with his face. Today, he listens and I talk.

Where did that laminated photo come from? I remembered it from years ago. Mark was sitting in a butterfly-type wing chair that he could lie back in yet not fall out of. Memories came flooding back. Talk about kindness, persistence, resilience and—

And what? The answer came with a casual flip-over of the laminated picture. There on the back were charcoal-penciled words in what was unmistakably Russ's handwriting. Not surprising that he would write on the back of Mark's picture, because to Russ, Mark was a true saint. Russ's scrupulous Catholicism made Mark as canonized as Saint Francis of Assisi. And then I read the inscription: "May the prayers of your brother Mark keep you safe and healthy. 8/24/69."

Damn! I was dumbfounded. I was in Vietnam in August 1969. My father had never hugged me or said "I love you." He couldn't. As I learned, with help, that was the best Russ could do. Unbelievable. He had sent that to me in Vietnam and I must have seen the picture, not the inscription, and tossed it in my duffle bag. If I did at that time read the inscription, I would have completely disregarded it and filed it away under "This doesn't change a goddamn thing with me, Russ." I suspect that the latter was the most likely.

Now, 50 years later, I understand. It must have hurt Russ more than my bypass surgery to reach inside and melt the wall, exposing himself. And yet he did. That one gesture said, "Tom, I love you and am proud of you. You are doing what I was never able to accomplish. I worry for you and put your safety in the hands of my greatest saint, your brother Mark." Russ too had a moment as a blade of grass in my stone wall, just as Ellen had.

Fifty years have passed. Fifty years of anger and questions. Fifty years of Ellen and Russ. Today they have taught me forgiveness, perhaps the most important sacrament for all of us to have in our relationships with others and ourselves.

Thank you, Mom and Dad.

The End
(Really? I don't think so!!)

May the prayers
of your brother,
Mark, keep
you safe
and in good
health.

8/24/69

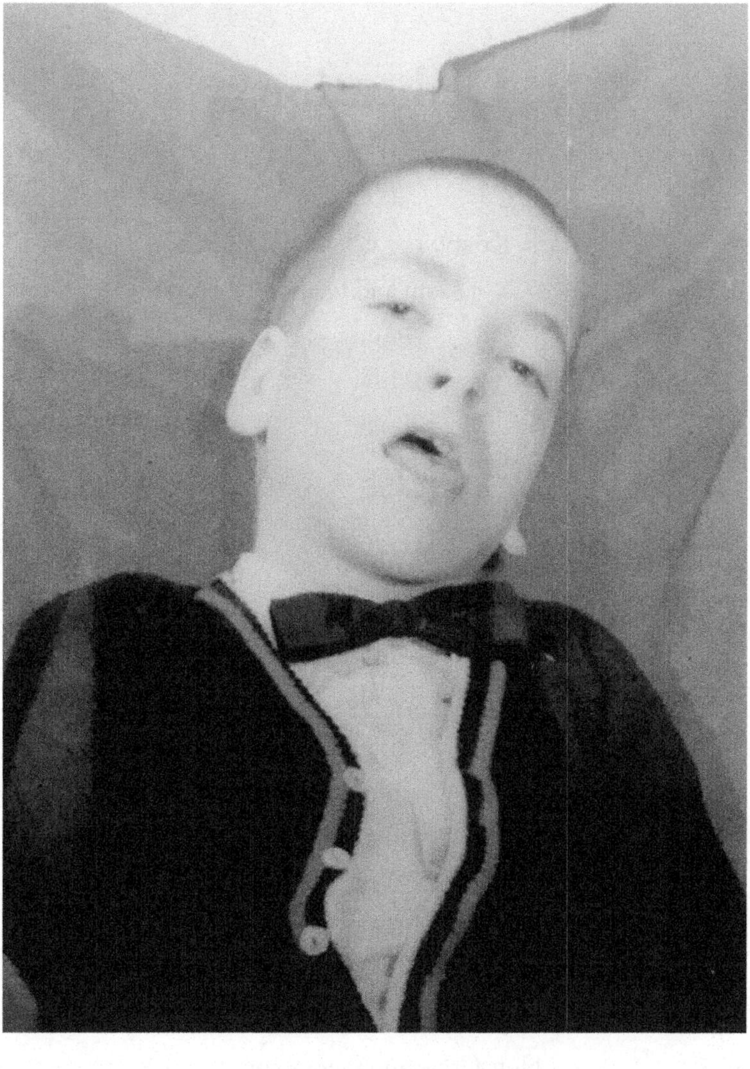

Dedication

Mark, Kristy, and Ellie, my children
Mom and Dad
Granny
Missy
Luke
Zoe
Zadie
William
Robert
Rob
Geoff
Sue
Jon
Russ
Oz
Dorann
Brendan
John A. and Kathleen
Holy Cross and Georgetown
All Those I've Neglected

Made in the USA
Monee, IL
05 April 2021

63784708R00132